Gabriel García Márquez's
Love in the Time of Cholera

Also available in this series:

Forthcoming in this series:

· GABRIEL GARCÍA MÁRQUEZ'S

Love in the Time of Cholera

A READER'S GUIDE

THOMAS FAHY

CONTINUUM | NEW YORK | LONDON

2003

The Continuum International Publishing Group Inc
370 Lexington Avenue, New York, NY 10017

The Continuum International Publishing Group Ltd
The Tower Building, 11 York Road, London SE1 7NX

www.continuumbooks.com

Copyright © 2003 by Thomas Fahy

Printed in the United States of America

Library of Congress Cataloging-in-Publication Data

Fahy, Thomas Richard.
    Gabriel García Márquez's Love in the time of cholera : a reader's guide / Thomas Fahy.
        p.   cm. — (Continuum contemporaries)
    Includes bibliographical references.
    ISBN 0-8264-1475-3 (pbk. : alk. paper)
    1. García Márquez, Gabriel, 1928– Amor en los tiempos del câolera.
I. Title.   II. Series.
PQ8180.17.A73A834   2003
863'.64 — dc21   2003003727

Contents

For my parents, Tom and Eileen Fahy,
and my brother, Michael

Acknowledgements

I am grateful to a number of people for their help with this book. Many thanks to Linda Wagner-Martin for her ongoing support and generosity. She continues to be a patient guide, caring mentor, and dear friend.

Without the tireless efforts of Kirstin Ringelberg and Fiona Mills, I'm not sure I would finish any project. You are inspirational friends and exceptional colleagues. Thank you.

Finally, I would like to thank Susann Cokal and Kathryn Rummell for their invaluable help and insightful feedback at the eleventh hour.

1

The Novelist

Gabriel José García Márquez once lamented to his friend, Colombian poet Álvaro Mutis: "I'll never write again." Though he had just completed two short books, *In Evil Hour* (1956) and *No One Writes to the Colonel* (1957), neither would be published until 1962. Neither sold more than 700 copies. And neither yielded any royalties. To make matters worse, he was suffering from severe writer's block. Between 1961 and 1964, his inability to produce any literary work left him increasingly frustrated and discouraged. The young novelist had reached the lowest point of his career.

Then, like Saul on the road to Damascus, García Márquez was struck by inspiration. While driving his family to Acapulco for a vacation in 1965, he suddenly knew what to write: "It was so ripe in me that I could have dictated the first chapter, word by word, to a typist."[1] He immediately turned the car around, put his wife Mercedes in charge of finances, and began to work. He wrote eight hours a day for eighteen months, and smoked so many cigarettes that his friends nicknamed his room "The Cave of the Mafia." In the mean-

---

[1] Mario Vargas Llosa, *García Márquez: Historia de un deicidio*, 75.

time, Mercedes secretly sold the car, pawned most of their house-hold goods (including an eggbeater), and borrowed money from friends to support the family. They were ten thousand dollars in debt by the time he emerged from "The Cave" with a thirteen-hundred page manuscript.

They immediately prepared the unwieldy text for his publisher in Argentina and walked to the post office—only to discover that they could not afford to mail it. So they sent the first half and returned later that day after Mercedes sold her hair dryer and an electric heater to pay postage for the rest of it. The novel, *One Hundred Years of Solitude*, would change their lives almost overnight. The initial 8,000 copies were sold within one week, and the novel continued to sell out for months. Within the first three years after its publication in 1967, 500,000 copies had been purchased. To date, the book has been translated into more than thirty languages and has sold around thirty million copies.

In many ways, this book was the culmination of García Már-quez's upbringing in the coastal region of northern Colombia. He once claimed: "I feel that all my writing has been about the experiences of the time I spent with my grandparents." From listening to stories about war heroes and local myths, he developed a deep ap-preciation for history, folklore, and South American culture. As both a journalist (which enabled him to write about the political turmoil of the country) and a voracious reader of classic and modernist liter-ature, García Márquez found a distinct literary voice that crystal-lized in *One Hundred Years of Solitude* and would continue to shape his writing.[2]

---

[2] The biographical material for this section is drawn primarily from Gene H. Bell-Villada's *García Márquez: The Man and His Work* (Chapel Hill: University of North Carolina Press, 1990), Jon Lee Anderson's "The Power of Gabriel García Márquez" (*The New Yorker*, Sept. 27, 1999), and the García Márquez website www.themodernword.com/gabo.

A Country in Turmoil

Gabriel García Márquez's art cannot be understood apart from the political and social history of Colombia. Since the mid-nineteenth century, Colombia has had a dual party political system, the Liberals and Conservatives. Traditionally, Liberals have opposed the church and centralized government, supported labor reform and social tolerance, and expanded individual rights. Years of bloody conflict, however, have blurred the ideological distinctions between these two groups, and their ruthless struggle for power continues to devastate the country today.

Several significant conflicts involving these groups appear throughout García Márquez's fiction. The War of a Thousand Days, which claimed over 100,000 lives, began in 1899 and lasted almost three years. This civil war was the culmination of political tensions in the nineteenth century and, until recently, was considered the most violent conflict in Colombia's history. Throughout his childhood, García Márquez heard countless, first-hand stories about this war from his Liberal grandfather and guardian, Colonel Nicolás Márquez.

The Banana Massacre of 1928 also had a significant impact on García Márquez's imagination. In 1894, the United Fruit Company began buying land in northern Colombia, including García Márquez's hometown of Aracataca. Within the first few decades of the twentieth century, the banana industry was crucial to the economy of this region, and the Boston-based company had become one of the largest exporters of bananas in the world. In October 1928, over 32,000 workers organized a strike to protest the deplorable working conditions and lack of benefits. They wanted to be paid in cash, not in credit at the company store. They wanted toilets. The wanted sanitary living conditions and decent housing. In response, the Conservative government sent in troops who indiscriminately shot demonstrators, killing hundreds.[3] Within the next few months, dozens of people "disappeared," and ultimately, the government denied the incident. García Márquez would later make this one of the culminating events in *One Hundred Years of Solitude*.

Lastly, the bloody civil war known as "La Violencia" (1946–1965) became the starting point for García Márquez's career as a journalist. On April 9, 1948, politician Jorge Eliécer Gaitán was assassinated in the streets of Bogotá. A member of the Liberal party during the Banana Massacre and champion of the poor, Gaitán had risked his career and life by forming a congressional committee to investigate the incident. He also preached the virtues of democracy and corporate responsibility, much to the consternation of both parties. Within the next twenty years, his public popularity increased, endowing him with a great deal of political power. In 1946, he split the Liberal party, which enabled the Conservatives to take power. Desperate to maintain their control, the Conservative party terrorized Liberal voters in subsequent elections, killing thousands within the year. In 1947, the Liberals regained control of Congress and immediately elected Gaitán as party leader.

Gaitán's murder on April 9, 1948 sparked fierce riots that lasted three days. In the end, 2,500 people were killed as a result of this explosive uprising, known more commonly as *El Bogotazo* ("The Bogotá Coup"). Both parties subsequently formed numerous guerrilla groups that conducted murderous raids. Women and children were slaughtered. Thousands of homes were destroyed or confiscated, which forced over a million peasants to flee to Venezuela. This unbridled violence tore apart the country for years. Eventually, the Conservatives dissolved the Liberal Congress in order to perse-

---

[3] Some estimates are significantly higher. Union leader Alberto Castrillón, for example, "would calculate the dead at Ciénga alone at 400; for the larger strike he estimated a total of 1,500 dead and 3,000 wounded" (Bell-Villada 105).

cute, hunt down, and kill the Liberals (who were labeled "Communists" at this time). By 1953, over 150,000 lives were lost.

Family Stories

Born on March 6, 1927, Gabriel García Márquez grew up in Aracataca, Colombia—a small village near the Caribbean Sea. His parents, Luisa Santiaga Márquez and Gabriel Eligio García, left Gabriel in the care of his maternal grandparents, in part, to assuage Colonel Nicolás Márquez's disapproval of their marriage. The Colonel, a veteran of The War of a Thousand Days and a staunch Liberal, did not want his daughter marrying a Conservative man of lower social standing. Despite the Colonel's efforts to undermine their courtship, Gabriel Eligio's persistence prevailed. He won Luisa's heart through countless letters, love songs, poems, and even telegrams. Their courtship would become the basis for the heartbreaking love story of Florentino Ariza and Fermina Daza in *Love in the Time of Cholera*.

As a result of this familial discord, Gabriel grew up in a bustling house with three aunts and countless relatives—cousins, nephews, the Colonel's illegitimate children, and grandchildren. The Colonel, in addition to being a local hero, was a captivating storyteller who regaled Gabriel with tales of his youth, family, civil war, and the Banana Massacre of 1928. At one time, he had killed a man in a duel and often remarked to his grandson: "You can't believe how a dead man weighs you down." This sentiment, like the trips he and young Gabriel took to the circus and to the stores of the United Fruit Company to see ice, would reappear imaginatively through the lives of the Buendía family in *One Hundred Years of Solitude*.

His grandmother, Tranquilina Iguarán Cotes, and her sisters were also prolific storytellers, but unlike the Colonel, they preferred tales that blurred the lines between fantasy and reality, the living and the dead. (His aunt Francisca even wove a shroud in preparation for her own death.) Though the Colonel often scoffed at their superstitions, advising his grandson not to listen, Gabriel was enchanted; his relationships with these women not only inspired his female fictional characters, but also gave them a depth that was uncharacteristic in Colombian fiction of the 1960s and 1970s.

In 1935, the Colonel died, and eight-year-old Gabriel was sent to live with his parents in Sucre, which would become the setting for the nameless, river-port towns in *No One Writes to the Colonel* and *Chronicle of a Death Foretold*. Almost immediately, he was sent to boarding school in Barranquilla. Shy and reserved, Gabriel was so serious that his classmates called him "The Old Man." Within a few years, he received a scholarship to attend Liceo Nacional de Zipaquirá, a Jesuit high school for the gifted just outside of Bogotá. The journey required a lengthy trip up the Magdalena river on a steamboat, and Gabriel would make this the setting for *Love in the Time of Cholera* over forty years later. This was Gabriel's first trip to Bogotá, and he wept at the sight of the gray, rainy industrial city.

He was far from the warm coastal towns of his youth.

Gabriel enjoyed his studies, particularly of the humanities, and his passion for literature and cartoons gave him a reputation as a "writer." After graduating in 1946, however, he succumbed to his parents' pressure to go to law school instead of becoming a journalist. Completely uninterested in law, he did poorly in school and preferred reading poetry while riding the streetcars of Bogotá and spending time in cafes with the local literati.

Then, three events changed his life: he met his future wife, abandoned law school to become a journalist, and read Franz Kafka.

While visiting his parents during his first year of law school, he met thirteen-year-old Mercedes Barcha Pardo, a striking girl of

Egyptian descent whose exotic appearance earned her the nickname "the sacred crocodile." They pledged their love for each other, and he proposed that year. Although they delayed the marriage until each had finished school, they remained committed for over a decade until their wedding in 1958. (They later had two sons: Rodrigo, born in 1959, and Gonzalo, born in 1962.)

Like so many Colombians, García Márquez was profoundly affected by the assassination of Jorge Gaitán in 1948, and even participated in the riots of *El Bogotazo*. García Márquez's boarding house was severely damaged by rioters who set a fire that destroyed most of his books and manuscripts. The University was quickly closed down after the incident. As a result, he transferred to the Universidad de Cartagena to complete his bachelor's degree. This move reconnected him with his Caribbean roots and his passion for journalism. While indifferently continuing with his studies of law, he began writing a five-hundred-word daily column for a local paper, *El Universal*. A case of pneumonia in 1949, however, interrupted both his studies and writing. But this sickness gave him time to read the works of Ernest Hemingway, William Faulkner, James Joyce, Virginia Woolf, and others. When he recovered, he decided to leave law school, move to Barranquilla, and take a job as a columnist for the coastal paper *El Heraldo* in 1950.

Literary Influences

Having spent the last four years reading literature on streetcars and in cafes, he discovered several writers who exposed him to possibilities he had not considered. García Márquez was particularly impressed by Franz Kafka's "The Metamorphosis": "When I read that I said to myself, 'Holy shit! Nobody'd ever told me you could do this!

So it *can* be done! Shit! That's how my grandma used to tell stories, the wildest things with a completely natural tone of voice.'"[4] García Márquez was captivated by the protagonist Gregor Samsa, who wakes up one morning to find "himself transformed in his bed into a gigantic insect" yet still struggles to get ready for work. Kafka's use of bizarre and extraordinary events in everyday settings recalled the storytelling of García Márquez's grandmother; and this would lay the groundwork for the magical world of Macondo in *One Hundred Years of Solitude*.

García Márquez also found an important model in William Faulkner, basing a number of his own narrative techniques on Faulkner's use of chronology (the seamless weaving of past and present) and the importance of geography (creating Yoknapatawpha County, a town with specific places and characters that recur throughout his works). In 1951, García Márquez stated: "my favorite authors for the moment are Faulkner, Kafka, and Virginia Woolf, and my fondest hope is to write as they do."[5] (He would later refer to "my master William Faulkner" in his 1982 Nobel Prize address.[6]) One of his earliest novels, *Leaf Storm*, for example, shares numerous similarities with *As I Lay Dying*—most obviously the multiple viewpoints and the central image of a coffin. And García Márquez's use of time and recurring names also parallels *The Sound and the Fury* and *Absalom, Absalom!*

As the epigraph of *Leaf Storm* suggests, García Márquez also admired the drama of Sophocles and was particularly intrigued by the ways in which *Oedipus Rex* foreshadowed and challenged the detec-

---

[4] Interview with *El Manifesto*, "El viaje a la semilla." In Renetería Mantilla, *García Márquez habla de García Márquez*, 161.

[5] Quoted in Bell-Villada, 81

[6] For a translated copy of García Márquez's Nobel Prize address "The Solitude of Latin America," see *Gabriel García Márquez: New Readings* (Cambridge, 1987): 207–211.

tive genre. García Márquez himself would play with these conventions in his tale of Santiago Nasar's murder in *Chronicle of a Death Foretold*. More importantly, however, García Márquez recognized parallels between the complexities of power in Greek tragedy and the dictatorships of the twentieth century. As biographer Gene H. Bell-Villada explains, "García Márquez has praised *Oedipus Rex* on numerous counts, singling it out above all as the work that taught him the most about power, a phenomenon that would obsess him and which he would masterfully dissect in *The Autumn of the Patriarch*" (73).

Another significant influence for García Márquez, particularly in regards to humor, was the writing of François Rabelais. Both share a cunning sense for the carnivalesque, irreverent, bawdy, and physical. The influence of Rabelais's satire on religious and political figures is clearly evident throughout García Márquez's oeuvre, including *In Evil Hour, One Hundred Years of Solitude,* and *Of Love and Other Demons*. Corrupt government officials, myopic priests, and hapless entrepreneurs crowd the pages of these texts and wonderfully illustrate the ways humor can enrich narrative.

The Long Wandering

Restless and struggling with his own fiction, García Márquez eventually quit his job with *El Heraldo* and moved back to Bogotá in 1954—after spending some time as a traveling encyclopedia salesman in 1953. Here, he started working for another newspaper, *El Espectador*. In 1955, a sailor named Luis Alejandro Velasco presented García Márquez with a story that re-ignited his passion for fiction and forced him to leave Colombia. Velasco was the only survivor of a Colombian naval vessel that supposedly sank from a violent storm on its way from Alabama to Cartagena. For ten days, the sailor survived without food or water in a raft before drifting ashore in Urabá. The Colombian government proclaimed Velasco a national hero and used his "story" of survival as propaganda. He made public addresses, participated in parades, and even advertised watches and shoes. But when he walked into the office of *El Espectador*, he was ready to tell the truth. The ship was carrying illegal cargo and sank because of the crew's carelessness and incompetence (in stowing contraband). García Márquez recast the account and published it serially over two weeks. (In 1970, it appeared in book form as *The Story of a Shipwrecked Sailor*.) The story caused such a sensation that the government shut down the paper in 1956.

Afraid of repercussions from the government, García Márquez fled the country and traveled to Europe. He spent time in France, Poland, Czechoslovakia, and attended film school in Rome for several months. Then in 1957, he visited the Soviet Union and Eastern Europe with friend Plinio Apuleyo Mendoza. His writings about this journey were later published as "Ninety Days Behind the Iron Curtain" in *Cromos*, a Bogotá magazine. Soon after their trip, Mendoza asked García Márquez to join the writing staff of *Momento*, a magazine in Caracas. His move to Venezuela coincided with the quick erosion of General Marcos Pérez Jiménez's power as dictator, and the eventual army uprising that overthrew him. During the collapse of this right-wing dictatorship and Fidel Castro's triumph over Fulgencio Batista's government in Cuba, García Márquez became interested in dictatorship, which would inspire him to write *The Autumn of the Patriarch* (1975). He even started writing for Castro's news agency, *Prensa Latina*, and began a life-long friendship with the Cuban leader during this period.

García Márquez, along with his wife and baby boy, left Havana and took a post in the New York branch of *Prensa Latina* in 1961. García Márquez eventually resigned as tensions between the United States and Cuba escalated, and he started receiving threatening phone calls at work. "In the aftermath of the Bay of Pigs invasion, hard-line pro-Soviet Cuban Communists took over many government posts, and Masetti resigned his position. García Márquez quit in solidarity with him, and he and Mercedes and the baby got on a bus headed south, to explore the world of William Faulkner."[7] They ended up in Mexico City, which has been their "home" ever since. During this time, he completed the stories that would be published as *Big Mama's Funeral* and revised both *No One Writes to the Colonel* and *In Evil Hour* (after changing its original title, "This Town of Shit"). In fact, *In Evil Hour* won the 1962 Esso Prize while it was still in manuscript form.

The Successful Years

After the astounding success of *One Hundred Years of Solitude* in 1967, García Márquez moved to Barcelona—in part to flee the barrage of fan mail and requests for interviews. He also wanted to live under a waning dictatorship in order to write *The Autumn of the Patriarch*, which would take seven years to complete. In addition to publishing *Innocent Eréndira and Other Stories* (1972) and a collection of journalistic writings *Cuando era feliz e indocumentado* ("When I Was Happy and Uninformed", 1973), he began using his fame and political clout as an activist during this period. Through writings and financial donations, he supported numerous left-wing causes in Colombia, Venezuela, Argentina, and Angola as well as groups such as Movimiento al Socialismo (MAS), the Committee in Solidarity with Political Prisoners, and HABEAS (a group dedicated to liberating political prisoners in Latin America).

In 1981, he returned to Colombia briefly and heard rumors that the government planned to arrest him. He had been accused of fi-

[7] See Anderson's "The Power of Gabriel García Márquez": 56–69.

nancing a group of M-19 guerrillas—an accusation that was exacerbated by his outspoken criticism of the government and his ties to Cuba. So he returned to Mexico and requested political asylum. In the same year, *Chronicle of a Death Foretold* was published, and a few months later, in 1982, the fifty-four-year-old author received the Nobel Prize, making him the youngest recipient since Albert Camus.

Internationally renowned and arguably one of the most important writers of the twentieth century, Gabriel García Márquez continues to write every day. He spends most of his time in Mexico City with his wife, but throughout the year they also travel to their other houses in Cuernavaca, Barcelona, Paris, Havana, Cartagena, and Barranquilla. "Each of them is furnished in the same way—with white carpets, large glass coffee tables, modern art, a carefully chosen sound system, and an identical Macintosh computer."[8] Each morning, after reading the paper, drinking coffee, and answering e-mail, he sits at his desk to write from ten until two-thirty in the afternoon. After that, he spends time with his family and friends.

Since the Nobel Prize, he has published several books and collections, including *Love in the Time of Cholera* (1985), which was published in August of that year, three months ahead of schedule. For the first edition, 1,200,000 copies were printed for release in Spanish America, and an additional 250,000 for the Spanish market.[9] This publication was followed by *The General and His Labyrinth* (1989) about Símon Bolívar, *Of Love and Other Demons* (1994), and most recently, a work of non-fiction, *News of a Kidnapping* (1996).

In 1999, a rumor began circulating on the internet claiming that Márquez had died. He did collapse from a mysterious illness in June

[8] Ibid. 58.

[9] Information about the publication of *Love in the Time of Cholera* is cited in Robin Fiddian's "A Prospective Post-Script: Apropos of *Love in the Time of Cholera*" from *Gabriel García Márquez: New Readings*: 191–205.

of that year (which also became highly exaggerated news on the internet) and spent a week in the hospital. But it wasn't until he checked himself into a hospital a few months later that he discovered the possible source for his fatigue and sickness. He was diagnosed with lymphatic cancer. Since then, he has received treatment and claims to feel stronger.

The works of Gabriel García Márquez have captured the imagination of people around the world for over thirty years. As an activist and an artist, he has asked people of all races and classes to examine the dangers of power, greed, selfishness, and indifference. And in the face of suffering, whether from death, sickness, injustice, or cruelty, his vision always seems to return to the healing power of love and compassion.

2

The Novel

Several years ago, a friend from college gave me a copy of Gabriel García Márquez's *Love in the Time of Cholera*. It was a wonderful surprise on an uneventful summer afternoon months away from any special occasion like a birthday or Christmas. It was just a gift inspired by the text, and it was my introduction to the author. In the inscription, she wrote: "I only hope there is someone out there that I will love with the same persistence and devotion as Florentino Ariza." Indeed, there is something admirable about Florentino's journey. His persistent, highly sentimentalized love for Fermina Daza appeals to many of our own desires to find a love that will last, as the last word of the novel suggests, "forever." Clearly, my friend, who is still searching for her own Florentino, found hope in his quest. But there is little to admire about Florentino himself. A callous, selfish man whose obsession with Fermina blinds him to the needs of others, Florentino has affairs with married women and teenage girls. He is even responsible for the deaths of two women — one is killed by her husband, the other commits suicide.

In fairness, most of the characters in this novel are complicated and problematic. They make mistakes and live with regrets. They fall in and out of love. They struggle with loneliness and belonging, desire and loss, fantasy and reality. We can only conclude, along with the narrator, that "nothing in the world [is] more difficult than love" (213).

The novel spans over a sixty year period, from approximately 1875 to 1935. (References to the premiere of Offenbach's *Tales of Hoffman* [1881] and a screening of the film *All Quiet on the Western Front* [1930] help establish this timeline.) The plot is driven by two love stories. While delivering a telegram to a local businessman named Lorenzo Daza, seventeen-year-old Florentino Ariza sees, and immediately falls in love with, his daughter, thirteen-year-old Fermina Daza. Florentino courts her with volumes of highly-sentimental letters, violin serenades, roses, and perfumes. After a year of "devastating love" (68), Fermina agrees to marry Florentino as long as he promises not to make her eat eggplant. Eventually, she rejects him because of her own disillusionment with his appearance after a prolonged separation.

Soon after this break, the scare of cholera brings the young, successful Dr. Juvenal Urbino to the Daza home, and he too becomes infatuated with Fermina. Unlike Florentino, Dr. Urbino comes from an aristocratic family, which appeals to Lorenzo's desire for his daughter to marry into a higher social class. Initially, Fermina resists the doctor's proclamations of love, but after her father's financial crisis, she consents to marry Urbino. Even though both recognize that they are not in love with each other on their wedding night, they begin a life and family together.

Meanwhile, Florentino, whose love never wanes for Fermina, begins working for his uncle's river-transport company. Over the years, he has affairs with at least 622 women and diligently climbs through the ranks of the company with one hope—that his success will one day make him worthy of Fermina's love. "Fifty-one years and nine months and four days" (105) later, Dr. Urbino dies, and Florentino brazenly proclaims his love for her that night: " 'I have waited for this opportunity for more than half a century, to repeat to you once again my vow of eternal fidelity and everlasting love' " (50). Though infuriated at first, she gradually begins a friendship with him that rekindles their love, and they consummate this relationship on a riverboat trip at the end of the novel.

As this story suggests, García Márquez is interested in exploring the intersection of love and time, particularly aging, and he achieves this, in part, through structural and stylistic devices. *Love in the Time of Cholera* is divided into six chapters that are told from one narrative perspective. These chapters establish three distinct time periods.

The first spans two years, when seventy-six-year-old Florentino Ariza renews his courtship with Fermina. The second covers over a fifty-year history, from their broken engagement until Dr. Urbino's death. Lastly, the narrator alludes to the Colonial and political history of Colombia, suggesting the destructive, long-term impact of violence and war on the country and those living in it. The entire story is set in an unnamed town in northern Colombia, probably Cartagena, near the Magdalena River. And it is along this river that we watch both the decay of the stately town and the evolution of Florentino's and Fermina's loves.

Stylistically, García Márquez models his text on a nineteenth-century Spanish literary form, the *folletín*. As he explained in an interview with Fançesc Arroyo, "I wanted to write a nineteenth-century novel [. . . similar to those] written in the nineteenth century, as if it were actually written at that time."[10] The *folletín*, a type of sentimental writing that was published serially (like the works of Charles Dickens in England or Harriet Beecher Stowe in the United States) typically includes a love triangle (like Fermina, Florentino,

---

[10] This discussion is reprinted in "El amor, la vejez, la muerte: un paseo con Gabriel García Márquez por la trama y la historia de su última novella," *El País* (*Libras*), Year 7, 321 (Madrid, 12 December 1985), 1–3.

and Urbino), features a love-poet as romantic hero (Florentino), re-
lies on unlikely coincidences ("that were common in the novels of
the day, but that no one believed in real life" [266]), uses clichés
about love (such as "There is no greater glory than to die for love"
[82]), presents a father who tries to make his daughter a "lady," etc.
These conventions are not so different from those found in contemporary soap operas, and they suit García Márquez's penchant for hy-
perbole and the fantastic.

Yet, as some of these examples suggest, he also uses the conventions to critique the dangers of idealizing love. By focusing on a cou-
ple in their seventies, García Márquez establishes a stark contrast
between the realities of the aging body (frailty, illness, forgetfulness,
incontinence, smell) and more youthful, romanticized visions of
sexual desire. In addition to this literary tradition, García Márquez
also modeled his text on two novels—Simone de Beauvoir's *The
Coming of Age* (also referred to as *Old Age*) and Gustave Flaubert's
Madame Bovary. The former explores the psychological impact of
aging. The latter deals with the tensions between private desire and
social propriety, disillusionment, the dangers of reading, and the
quest for power.

Two personal events also inspired the writing of this novel. While
researching *Love in the Time of Cholera*, García Márquez discovered that his seventy-year-old parents "were still—at that time—
making love!"[11] Like Florentino, his father played the violin and had
worked as a telegraph operator in his youth. And Colonel Nicolás
Márquez, Luisa's father and Gabriel's mother, opposed her relationship and marriage to Eligio. The second influence on the novel was
a newspaper article that García Márquez read in the 1960s about an
affair between two Americans. Each were happily married, but they
met secretly in Acapulco once a year for decades. This affair was

---

[11] See Pete Hamill's "Love and Solitude." *Vanity Fair*, March 1988: 192.

discovered only after a boatman murdered the seventy-year-old cou-
ple and stole their money. At the end of the novel, Fermina hears of
a similar story on the radio and is profoundly affected by it. "Fermina Daza, who never cried over the soap operas on the radio, had
to hold back the knot of tears that choked her" (318).

This article not only illustrates the erotic desire that exists among
the elderly, but it also makes a disturbing connection between passion and violence. García Márquez once stated that "what matters
to me most [in *Love in the Time of Cholera*] is the analysis it conducts of love at all ages."[12] Certainly, love is the nexus that links
characters, settings, memories, and time throughout the text, but this
novel is much more than a love story. Fermina Daza's life-long relationships with both Dr. Juvenal Urbino and Florentino Ariza are
complicated by class, modernity, illness, sexual desire, violence (associated with politics and war), age, and ethnicity.

This section will explore the various ways these forces intersect
with love and desire, and in doing so, will hopefully provide a critical apparatus for this remarkable and highly seductive text. García
Márquez, whose elegant prose often lulls us into the beautiful and
nostalgic aspects of this love story, has constructed a novel that is
quite dark and complex. Like Nabokov, whose style tempts us to
sympathize with the vile, perverted Humbert Humbert in *Lolita*,
García Márquez challenges us to look beyond the surface beauty of
language and face the wonderful, strained, magical, hurtful, and oftentimes devastating dimensions of love.

Not Quite Good Enough

Throughout *Love in the Time of Cholera*, class defines people and
establishes the parameters for socially acceptable relationships. Dr.

---

[12] See "El amor, la vejez, la muerte: un paseo con Gabriel García Márquez por
la trama y la historia de su última novella," *El País* (*Libras*), Year 7, 321 (Madrid, 12
December 1985), 1–3.

Juvenal Urbino, for example, wears his aristocratic origins like a badge—distinguishing himself from his fellow citizens in every possible way. Not surprisingly, this becomes a source of contention in the town: "He was not only the city's oldest and most illustrious physician, he was also its most fastidious man. Still, his too obvious display of learning and the disingenuous manner in which he used the power of his name had won him less affection than he deserved" (5).

This lack of affection is not merely felt among the lower classes. In fact, being "an expensive and exclusive doctor" keeps him from the poorest sectors of society most of the time. It is his treatment of the upper classes as "subordinates" that causes the greatest resentment. Even though most of his patients "were concentrated in the ancestral homes of the District of the Viceroys" (10), Urbino sees himself as above them. He is an aristocrat, not one of the ever-growing *nouveau-riche*, and his off-putting displays of social status, such as the conspicuous presence of his horse-drawn carriage, are a constant reminder of this distinction.

Dr. Urbino's was the only horse-drawn carriage; it was distinguishable from the handful left in the city because the patent-leather roof was always kept polished, and it had fittings of bronze that would not be corroded by salt, and wheels and poles painted red with gilt trimming like gala nights at the Vienna Opera. Furthermore, while the most demanding families were satisfied if their drivers had a clean shirt, he still required his coachman to wear livery of faded velvet and a top hat like a circus ringmaster's. (12)

Urbino's attitudes about class are so rooted in the past that they border on ridiculous, such as making his driver dress like a circus figure. Yet, like his elegant clothing and knowledge of Latin, they reflect his sense of self. His association with Europe further reinforces this self-imposed distance between himself and those around him. Urbino has a clear affection for all things European. He honeymoons with Fermina in Europe, and they vacation abroad several times throughout their marriage. More importantly, Urbino studied medicine and surgery in Paris before returning to his hometown, and this advanced (modern) training often sets him at odds with the "atavistic superstitions" (108) of the townspeople. "He was in conflict with everything: his renovating spirit, his maniacal sense of civic duty, his slow humor in a land of immortal pranksters—everything" (108).

Like the man himself, Urbino's house also "stood in another time" (18), and Fermina, who managed the home, gradually makes class an integral part of her identity. As a young girl, she seems impervious to her socially ambitious father, whose displeasure with Florentino is entirely about social position. As he tells Florentino in an attempt to intimidate him, "'the only thing worse than bad health is a bad name'" (81). After Fermina breaks their engagement, however, her father's financial difficulties seem to influence her decision to marry Urbino. Initially, their married life thrusts her into an unfamiliar social world: "Nothing happened without them: civic exhibitions, the Poetic Festival, artistic events, charity raffles, patriotic ceremonies, the first journey in a balloon" (212). And these responsibilities, as well as the gossip of jealous townswomen who resented her social climbing, weighed on her. "Life in [this] world [. . .] was nothing more than a system of atavistic contracts, banal ceremonies, preordained words, with which people entertained each other in society in order not to commit murder" (211). She even wonders at times if "she would have been happier with [Florentino], alone with him in that house she had restored for him with as much love as he had felt when he restored his house for her" (212).

By the time she learns of her husband's affair (and his confession to a priest), however, she has fully internalized this new class: "She was sure that her honor was the subject of gossip even before her husband had finished his penance, and the feeling of humiliation that this produced in her was much less tolerable than the shame and anger and injustice caused by his infidelity" (250). In other words, the shame of public humiliation and scandal—the kind that threaten the upper classes through the tabloids and local gossip—pains her more than the affair itself. Even Florentino recognizes this preoccupation with class when he plans to renew their courtship after fifty years: "It [his plan to win her affections] had to be a mad dream, one that would give her the courage she would need to discard the prejudices of a class that had not always been hers but had become hers more than anyone's" (293). To Florentino and arguably the rest of the town, she has become a consummate aristocrat. Not surprisingly, his "battle" plan does not free her to love him. Fermina actually conducts their relationship in secret to "keep up" social appearances. "Despite her unimpeachable life, Fermina Daza was more careful now than ever of everything she said or did, even with her closest friends. So that she maintained her connection to Florentino Ariza by means of the anachronistic thread of letters" (315). Fermina's romantic boundaries are clearly defined by class.

After her husband's death, however, two scandalous stories are published that erode these social proprieties and devastate Fermina, showing that she was "not immune to the hazards of her class" (319). The first story claimed an "alleged secret love affair between Dr. Juvenal Urbino and Lucrecia del Real Obispo. [. . . and] fell like a thundering cataclysm on the enfeebled local aristocracy. Not a line of it was true." (318–19). Honesty, like the reality of Uribino's affair, matters less than public image, and from this perspective, Fermina assumes Lucrecia's guilt when she stops visiting. (Lucrecia feels the same shame but doesn't have any other way to respond within the confines of her class.)

The second article accused Fermina's father of illegal business dealings, including extortion, counterfeiting, and selling arms (to, among others, author Joseph Conrad). In both cases, the implied notoriety undermines the image and social posturing that she has cultivated throughout her married life. Not surprisingly, these attacks "annihilated her [. . .]. Her decision not to go on living was evident in every gesture" (321). This response reflects her complete embodiment of aristocratic life and its emphasis, at least in this text, on public image. Even during the most difficult time in her marriage, the public relationship between Fermina and her husband was the glue that held them together: "The most absurd element in their situation was that they never seemed so happy in public as during those years of misery" (211). Only after these scandalous articles, when public humiliation shatters the last vestiges of her social propriety, is Fermina able to accept and love Florentino.

Florentino, though marginalized from both upper class and aristocratic circles, embodies a romanticized version of them. Regardless of the weather, he dresses like a gentleman out of a nineteenth-century romance novel: "he wore a romantic old-fashioned mustache with waxed tips. [. . .] a dark suit with a vest, a silk bow tie and a celluloid collar, a felt hat, and a shiny black umbrella that he also used as a walking stick" (48). Like his clothing suggests, Florentino clings desperately to the past, reading syrupy literature ("[preferring] the worst to the best" [167]), making "furious" love with hundreds of women (believing "that his illusory love for Fermina Daza could be replaced by an earthly passion" [143]), and writing poetry. In fact, he sees the world in such highly sentimentalized terms that he is unable to write business documents for the riverboat company: "Florentino Ariza wrote everything with so much passion that even official documents seemed to be about love. His bills of lading were rhymed no matter how he tried to avoid it, and routine business letters had a lyrical spirit that diminished their authority" (167). As a result, he starts composing love letters for other people after work, "helping unlettered lovers express their scented love notes, in order to unburden his heart of all the words of love that he could not use in customs reports" (168). All of these writings are about Fermina to some extent. Though he would prefer writing sentimental poetry and thinly-veiled fiction about his sexual exploits, he continues to work diligently at the riverboat company ("no matter how hard or humiliating" [168]), for "winning back Fermina Daza was the sole purpose of his life" (173). He believes that financial success in a prominent position, like his uncle's, will make him a socially acceptable suitor for Fermina.

Florentino is reminded of his lower social status long after his rise to the top of the company. When Dr. Urbino Daza (Fermina and Juvenal's son) invites him to lunch at the Social Club, Florentino recalls being previously excluded from this place. "The Social Club reserved the right to refuse admission for any number of reasons, and one of the most important was illegitimate birth. [. . .] Florentino Ariza himself had suffered the humiliation of being asked to leave when he was already sitting at the table as the guest of one of the founding members" (311). With the young doctor, Florentino takes a chance and is admitted, "although he was not asked to sign the gold book for notable guests" (311). This reluctant acceptance once again serves as a reminder to Florentino about his place outside of aristocratic circles.

At the end of the novel, the river becomes an ideal space for their rekindled love, in part, because issues of class (as related to bloodline) don't exist on the boat *New Fidelity*. Somewhat ironically, Florentino has helped fashion a social hierarchy onboard. He ordered, for example, a "Presidential Suite" built for "high-ranking officials and very special guests [. . .] but his private conviction was that sooner or later it was going to be the joyous refuge of his wedding trip with Fermina Daza" (326). Descriptions of the elegant meals and private dining quarters also suggest a structure that privileges both those with money and those affiliated with the company. Despite the ways that class operates both in town and on the *New Fidelity*, this trip does provide Fermina and Florentino with new freedoms. They are free from the prying eyes of the tabloids, community gossip, and most of all, prejudices about sexual desire among the elderly. As Ofelia, Fermina's daughter shouts in frustration, "'love is ridiculous at our age [. . .] but at theirs it is revolting'" (323). Florentino, who has spent a lifetime living and loving without concern for public opinion, rejects such an attitude. (He is even able to disregard Dr. Urbino Daza's attitude that anyone over seventy should be sent to a nursing home to "be spared the humiliation, suffering, and frightful loneliness of old age" [312].) In the final moments of the novel, therefore, it is not surprising when Florentino orders the captain not to dock, but to turn around once again:

> "And how long do you think we can keep up this goddamn coming and going?" he asked.
> Florentino Ariza had kept his answer ready for fifty-three years, seven months, and eleven days and nights.
> "Forever," he said. (348)

The Perils of Modernity

Throughout *Love in the Time of Cholera*, García Márquez suggests that modernization is often at odds with both love (or at least romantic idealizations of love) and culture. He establishes this tension, in part, by juxtaposing Florentino, an embodiment of the nineteenth-century romantic, with Dr. Urbino, a representative of modern development and social progress. Though García Márquez is wary of both extremes, he presents Urbino's obsessive need to modernize as particularly dangerous—blinding him to the deleterious impact of technological development. Scholar Mabel Moraña sees this coexistence between modernization and violence as reflecting a critique of modernity. "[The author's critique] thus takes the form of loyalty to the past, to individualism, the questioning of the effects of modernizing praxis, and a defense of national identity" (41). García Márquez specifically invites readers to question the notion of modern "progress" by linking it with decimated landscapes and disillusionment.

In the final days of his life, Dr. Urbino reflects on the continued deterioration of the city. The infrastructure of both poor and rich neighborhoods suggests stagnation and decay, failure and loss. While driving through the old slave quarter, for example, he notes the horrendous living conditions:

> For the city, his city, stood unchanging on the edge of time: the same burning dry city of his nocturnal terrors and the solitary pleasure of puberty, where flowers rusted and salt corroded, where nothing had happened for four centuries except a slow aging among withered laurels and putrefying swamps. [. . .] Independence from Spain and then the abolition of slavery precipitated the conditions of honorable decadence in which Dr. Juvenal Urbino had been born and raised. The great old families sank into their ruined palaces in silence. [. . .] And so the very life of the colonial city, which the young Juvenal Urbino tended to idealize in his Parisian melancholy, was an illusion of memory. In the eighteenth century, the commerce of the city had been the most prosperous in the Caribbean, owing in the main to the thankless privilege of its being the largest African slave market in the Americas. (16–18)

Urbino claims to be frustrated with the "unchanging" quality of the city, but in fact, the city has changed. In its history, it has broken away from colonial rule and the slave trade, but these things have only destroyed the aristocratic world that Urbino values. For him, the city stagnates because of its failure both to maintain social hierarchies and to embrace European ideas of progress. After returning from his medical studies in Paris, for example, he only sees decay: "Everything seemed smaller to him than when he left, poorer and sadder, and there were so many hungry rats in the rubbish heaps of the streets that the carriage horses stumbled in freight" (106–7). He concludes in a moment of frustration: "'How noble this city must be [. . .] for we have spent four hundred years trying to finish it off and we still have not succeeded'" (111). Inspired by his education and urbanity, he takes it upon himself to change not only the city, but the culture that seems so resistant to modernization.

Despite instituting many important civic changes, Urbino cannot alter the cultural practices that perpetuate these problems. He initially gets the "highest authorities" to clean the drinking water, fill the sewers, and make the marketplace more sanitary. Yet he still feels disconnected from the people. "He was in conflict with everything: his renovating spirit, his maniacal sense of civic duty, his slow humor in a land of immortal pranksters—everything, in fact, that constituted his most estimable virtues provoked the resentment of his older colleagues and the sly jokes of the younger ones" (108).

Arguably, it is both his renovating spirit and aristocratic snobbery that distance him from the rest of the city. He cannot convince others to share his beliefs, in part, because he is no longer one of them. This is particularly evident in his unwillingness to assist poor patients: "He was always an expensive and exclusive doctor, and his patients were concentrated in the ancestral homes in the District of the Viceroys" (10). Thus, Urbino's investment in both a strict class structure and modern "progress" calls into question the altruism of his civic works. He even abuses his position of prominence on occasion. As the president of the Society for Public Improvement, which founded the first fire department, Urbino calls on them to get his parrot out of a tree. "'Tell them it's for me'" (25). His status gives him privileges unavailable to most, and he readily takes advantage of them.

Fermina, on the other hand, resents the ways that technology and modernization have changed the land. When she visits her father's family in San Juan de la Ciénaga, she is shocked at its transformation:

Then Fermina saw her town again in the somnolence of two o'clock in the afternoon. She saw the streets that seemed more like beaches with scum-covered pools, and she saw the mansions of the Portuguese, with their coats of arms carved over the entrance and bronze jalousies at the windows. [. . .] She saw the deserted plaza, with no trees growing in the burning lumps of sodium nitrate, the line of carriages with their funereal tops and their horses asleep where they stood, the yellow train to San Pedro Alejandrino [. . .]. She drove around and around, but she could not recognize the old family house, for where she supposed it to be she found only a pigsty, and around the corner was a street lined with brothels where whores from all over the world took their siestas in the doorways in case there was something for them in the mail. It was not the same town. (252)

Modernity in its many forms (trains, ships, mail, an international community) has only made the town arid, dirty, and lifeless. Ethnic cultures (Spanish and South American) remain separate and distinct. It is a place where sex is found in prostitution, where international trade has brought "whores from all over the world," and where the distinction between rich and poor is brutally clear. These changes not only clash with Fermina's memories of home, but they also make her recognize certain truths about her own body. When visiting Cousin Hildebranda, she sees the ways in which time has effected each of them physically. "It was as if she were seeing herself in the mirror of truth. She was fat and old, burdened with unruly children [. . .]. But she was still the same person inside her ruined body" (253). Fermina clearly wants to see beyond the literal (her "ruined" body and the filthy streets); she wants to believe that certain things will always remain the same.

After Urbino's death, however, Fermina discovers how these changes (whether brought on by modernization or neglect) threaten to consume the past. Her memories of Florentino and the park where he used to court her are slipping away. "She tried to remember just how the little park was then, and the shabby almond trees,

and the bench where he had loved her, because none of it still ex-
isted as it had been then. They had changed everything, they had
removed the trees with their carpet of yellow leaves and replaced the
statue of the decapitated hero with that of another [. . .]. Her house,
sold many years before, had fallen into total ruin at the hands of the
Provincial Government" (282). Throughout the novel, the government is responsible for both the incessant modernization of the
country as well as its gradual decline. Furthermore, the link between
modernization and Fermina's inability to remember this youthful
love also suggests that love is not immutable. Time and modernization can change the heart as well as the landscape.

Even though Florentino embodies the past, he works for his uncle's riverboat company (a place associated with modern progress),
and García Márquez associates this industry with decay and loss.
Even Florentino's initial impressions highlight this decay and destruction:

[. . .] it was a dusty shed of no definite color, and on the rusting roof there
were patches of new tin plates over the original ones. [. . .] at the back there
was a closed sewer pipe, dirty and foul-smelling, where the refuse of a half
century of river navigation lay rotting: the debris of historic boats, from the
early one with a single smokestack [. . .] to some so recent that they had
electric fans in the cabins. Most of them had been dismantled for material
to be used in building other boats, but many were in such good condition
that it seemed possible to give them a coat of paint and launch them without
frightening away the iguanas or disturbing the foliate of the large yellow
flowers that made them even more nostalgic. (184)

Every aspect of this description signals waste. The ongoing proc-
ess of dismantling and rebuilding happens regardless of utility. New
ships are built simply for the sake of building something new—even
though these products quickly become garbage. This rebuilding

clearly doesn't improve anything. Boats still rot in a yard that smells like refuse from a closed sewer pipe.

The deleterious impact of this continual destroying and rebuilding is also evident in the destruction of the river. When Florentino and Fermina take their cruise along the Magdalena River at the end of the novel, Florentino witnesses the company's long-term impact on the environment: "Captain Samaritano explained to them how fifty years of uncontrolled deforestation had destroyed the river: the boilers of the riverboats had consumed the thick forest of colossal trees [. . .]. The hunters for skins from the tanneries in New Orleans had exterminated the alligators [. . .]. The parrots with their shrieking and the monkeys with their lunatic screams had died out as the foliage was destroyed" (331). Technology and the men responsible for it ravage the landscape. The company cuts down trees to fuel the boilers; hunters kill animals for sport and profit. These images suggest that modern technology only takes in. It does not replenish. Fermina and Florentino notice a dearth of animals and several abandoned towns along the river. People have fled these places as a result of modernization and industry. Florentino and Fermina ironically attempt to escape such realities (even though Florentino has helped contribute to them) through their trip. But García Márquez suggests that the devastation is too widespread to ignore. Even as they prepare to go back ashore, the ship must navigate "around the wrecks of boats and the platforms of oil wells in the bay [. . .] Fermina Daza could not bear the pestilential stink of [the city's] glories" (346). The modern realities of home and the river clash with Fermina's nostalgia and idealizations of the land. The modern world has left a trail of waste that ravages both land and memory.

A Time of Cholera

García Márquez's fascination with plagues can be traced back to his early interest in the writings of Albert Camus. He also did a considerable amount of research in preparation for *Love in the Time of Cholera*, and this historical framework gives the text its realistic quality. As with class and modernization, García Márquez links cholera with love, suggesting that both can be equally destructive.

Scholar Manuel Martinez-Maldonado has examined some of the historical components of the text, highlighting 1832 and 1866 as two significant years. Both dates refer to cholera epidemics that spread to the Caribbean. "Infected passengers also came directly from Europe or traveled in boats from New Orleans to the French or British colonies in the Caribbean basin—Martinique, Guadaloupe, the French Guyana, Jamaica" (131). At different points in the text, Urbino and Florentino notice ships from both New Orleans and Jamaica. Florentino actually witnesses the yellow flag of the plague during his first riverboat trip: "But that same day they encountered another boat, with a cargo of cattle for Jamaica, and were informed that the vessel with the plague flag was carrying two people sick with cholera, and that the epidemic was wreaking havoc along the portion of the river they still had to travel" (141). The river, which carries people, animals, and cargo, also carries a devastating disease. As Martinez-Maldonado explains, "it is well known that by 1865 cholera had established itself in the West Indies. Boats from Europe, an unquestionable source of contagion, were a main source of supplies to the Spanish and British colonies in the area" (131). Florentino's fears of contagion arguably reflect those felt by most of the characters at one time or another. People witness disease-ridden bodies floating down the river. Parents fear for their children. And even the pangs of love get confused for the symptoms of cholera.

Other details in the novel also allude to actual nineteenth-century epidemics and practices. Dr. Urbino's approach to fighting cholera, for example, is modeled on Robert Koch, the scientist who first discovered *vibrio comma* (the bacteria causing Asiatic cholera). Koch believed that clean drinking water and better sanitation practices were the best means for preventing widespread contagion. Along with other doctors, he raced to fight the scope and speed of these epidemics. "The first great Western cholera epidemics began in 1817, when the bacillus traveled by ship and caravan from its endemic site in the Ganges to Europe as far as England. From there it spread to the Americas and, in 1832, killed 5000 people in New Orleans. [. . .] In the same decade [1870s] that the fictional Urbino is pioneering sanitary improvements in Latin America, cholera killed 8600 persons in Hamburg" (Martinez-Maldonado, 130, 131). García Márquez not only draws on this history to establish Urbino's obsession with cholera but also to expose the social ramifications associated with it. Blacks and the poor were typically blamed for carrying the disease, while cases of cholera among the upper classes were either covered up or attributed to other illnesses. Similar attitudes are apparent in the novel. Urbino, for example, felt "alarmed at the possibility that the plague had entered the sanctuary of the old city, for all the cases until that time had occurred in the poor neighborhoods, and almost all of those among the black population" (115–16). Once again, Urbino's assumptions about the physical and social superiority of the upper classes make the possibility of cholera in those circles unthinkable. He is even convinced that the Daza home must be "immune to the plague" (116).

By linking the symptoms of cholera with love, García Márquez depicts love as a merciless, even violent force. Both cause headaches, nausea, stomachaches, fever, and dizziness. Early in the novel, Tránsito thinks that her son, Florentino, has cholera. "He lost his voice and his appetite and spent the entire night tossing and turning in his bed. [. . . His] anguish was complicated by diarrhea and green vomit; he became disoriented and suffered from sudden fainting spells, and his mother was terrified because his condition did not resemble the turmoil of love so much as the devastation of cholera" (61). A local doctor quickly dismisses these concerns, how-

ever. "All that was needed was shrewd questioning, first of the patient and then of his mother, to conclude once again that the
symptoms of love were the same as those of cholera" (62). The
phrase "once again" implies that this is a fairly common mistake.
And several times throughout the novel, people misinterpret Florentino's love sickness for cholera. In an interesting inversion of this association between cholera and love, Florentino pretends to have the
disease at the end of the novel. He orders the captain to raise the
plague flag in the final moments of the cruise, thus continuing the
trip "without stopping, without cargo or passengers, without coming
into any port" (342). He hopes this deception will insulate his love
for Fermina from the rest of the world, and he justifies it in the name
of love. "Besides, many times in the history of the river the yellow
plague flag had been flown in order to evade taxes, or to avoid pick-
ing up an undesirable passenger [. . .]. If such things were done for
so many immoral, even contemptible reasons, Florentino Ariza
could not see why it would not be legitimate to do them for love"
(343). This legerdemain seems fitting. Both forces seize their victims
unexpectedly; both cause suffering; and both can lead to death.

Dr. Urbino tries to control both cholera and love, but despite his
successes against the disease, the love of two women (Fermina Daza
and Miss Barbara Lynch) has the power to incapacitate him. Not
surprisingly, the fear of illness introduces him to each of them, but
instead of discovering anything serious, like cholera in the case of
Fermina, he finds a passion that unmoors him from his typical control and reserve—though only temporarily. He is first summoned to
the Daza house because another doctor is concerned that Fermina
has contracted cholera. Almost immediately, he falls in love. At this
moment, he could claim "victory" over the cholera epidemic in the
region, but "he was distracted and in disarray and ready to forget
everything else in life, because he had been struck by the lightning
of his love for Fermina Daza" (115). Early in their courtship, Urbino

does regain control over his infatuation, and on their wedding night, "he was aware that he did not love her. He had married her because he liked her haughtiness, her seriousness, her strength, and also because of some vanity on his part" (159). The nature of Urbino's and Fermina's love remains ambiguous throughout their lives, and this can be attributed in part to the control that they *both* exert over their feelings: "Neither could have said if their mutual dependence was based on love or convenience, but they had never asked the question with their hands on their hearts because both had always preferred not to know the answer" (26).

Nevertheless, Urbino is overcome by love (or at least infatuation) when he first meets Fermina; in other words, love momentarily exercises a power over him that he cannot control. This happens again with another woman during his marriage, and the affair almost destroys their relationship. It certainly devastates Fermina for a time: "She was suffering, and she resolved that the only way she could keep from dying was to burn out the nest of vipers that was poisoning her soul" (240). Urbino first met Barbara Lynch at the clinic of Misericordia Hospital, and "he knew almost immediately that something irreparable had just occurred in his destiny. She was tall, elegant, large-boned mulatta, with skin the color and softness of molasses. [. . .] Her sex seemed more pronounced than that of other human beings" (240–241). Early in his marriage, Urbino had been warned "that sooner or later he would have to confront a mad passion that could endanger the stability of his marriage," but he, "who thought he knew himself, knew the strength of his moral roots," (241) scoffed at the idea until he met Barbara. This love becomes so consuming that it makes him physically ill:

All the real or imaginary symptoms of his older patients made their appearance in his body. He felt the shape of his liver with such clarity that he could tell its size without touching it. He felt the dozing cat's purr of his kidneys, he felt the iridescent brilliance of his vesicles, he felt the humming blood in his arteries. At times he awoke at dawn gasping for air, like a fish out of water. He had fluid in his heart. [. . .] He went mad with terror. (247)

Even though Urbino attributes this more to a guilty conscience than to passion, his physical suffering is similar to Florentino's cholera-like symptoms for Fermina. Both men suffer because of love and passion. Both men, like so many of the characters in the novel, become infected by love and its oftentimes devastating consequences.

"My Heart Has More Rooms Than a Whorehouse"

García Márquez presents sex as a problematic, if not completely unreliable, way to express and interpret love. As one of Floretino's lovers explains: "spiritual love from the waist up and physical love from the waist down" (199). The tension surrounding this distinction is evident in our admiration for Florentino's undying commitment to Fermina—despite his deplorable treatment of women. By enticing us to root for Florentino, García Márquez suggests that we, like many of Florentino's conquests, are deceived by romance. Beyond García Márquez's seductive prose and Florentino's hyperbolic romanticism, men and women suffer—sometimes violently—at the hands of passion and sexual desire.

In many of Florentino's 622 affairs, sex is divorced from love—acting more as a salve for loneliness and longing. He sees the "earthly passion" (143) of sex as so far removed from his transcendent love for Fermina that he considers himself completely dedicated to her: "he always behaved as if he were the eternal husband of Fermina Daza, an unfaithful husband but a tenacious one, who fought endlessly to free himself from his servitude without causing her the displeasure of a betrayal" (197). When they finally consummate their relationship after fifty-three years, he exclaims: "'I've remained a virgin for you'" (339). Florentino clearly disassociates sex and love in order to justify his behavior with other women. At times, he cannot tell if his "habit of fornicating without hope was a mental necessity or a simple vice of the body" (174). Either way, he pursues sex tirelessly.

> No sooner did he leave his office, at five in the afternoon, than he began to hunt like a chicken hawk. At first he was content with what the night provided. He picked up serving girls in the parks, black women in the market, sophisticated young ladies from the interior on the beaches, gringas on the boats from New Orleans. He took them to jetties where half the city also went after nightfall, he took them wherever he could, and sometimes even where he could not, and not infrequently he had to hurry into a dark entryway and do what he could, however he could do it, behind the gate. (175)

Despite this description, Florentino convinces himself that he experiences love with these partners: "With her Florentino Ariza learned what he had already experienced many times without realizing it: that one can be in love with several people at the same time, feel the same sorrow with each, and not betray any of them. [. . .] 'My heart has more rooms than a whorehouse'" (270). But this idea is at odds with his behavior, and the reader has to be careful not to take Florentino (a great seducer and manipulator of language) at his word. This is not to say that all of his lovers are victims. Both men and women use sex to forget about painful experiences and past wrongs—"to find solace" (152). But in the case of Florentino Ariza, he is never completely honest with his lovers about his feelings for Fermina, and this deception ultimately reflects his selfishness and cruelty.

From the outset of the novel, García Márquez complicates our relationship to Florentino by suggesting that women love him more out of pity than desire. In his youth, Florentino was "the most sought-after young man in his social circle, the one who knew how to dance the latest dances and recite sentimental poetry by heart, and who was always willing to play violin serenades to his friends' sweethearts" (54). Yet he was far from an "ideal" lover physically. "He was very thin, with Indian hair plastered down with scented pomade and eyeglasses for myopia, which added to his forlorn appearance. Aside from his defective vision, he suffered from chronic constipation, which forced him to take enemas throughout his life" (54). Florentino certainly can't compare to the dapper Juvenal Urbino, but many women are attracted to his pitiable appearance and disposition. Fermina often laments, for example, "Poor man!" (206), and Hildebranda feels that "he is ugly and sad [. . .] but he is all love" (129). He is also described as "a wandering succubus" (303) and "a man passing through" (198) with a "helpless appearance" (168). In fact, hundreds of women have affairs with him out of pity, not sexual desire. They "promptly identified him as a solitary man in need of love, a street beggar as humble as a whipped dog, who made them yield without conditions, without asking him for anything, without hoping for anything from him except the tranquility of knowing they had done him a favor" (152). It is empathy and compassion—not love—that motivates sex, but even these emotions are more than Florentino offers in return.

Two of these affairs illustrate Florentino's selfish and callous use of sex. When he first meets Olimpia Zuleta, for example, Florentino sees himself as "the lover who never showed his face, the man most avid for love as well as most niggardly with it, the man who gave nothing and wanted everything" (216). He initially describes Olimpia as forgettable and not particularly attractive. But after witnessing her husband's thievery on the dock, he decides to seduce her: "A few days later he saw her husband at the port, loading merchandize instead of unloading it, and when the ship weighed anchor Florentino heard, with great clarity, the voice of the devil in his ear" (215).

Whether motivated by an odd sense of revenge (since he practically runs the riverboat company at this point) or mere perversity, Florentino courts her relentlessly to even the score. Olimpia finally yields after several months, and they have sex in a cabin on a riverboat. While lying naked afterwards, Florentino has a moment of "inspiration." He "opened a can of red paint that was within reach of the bunk, wet his index finger, and painted the pubis of the beautiful pigeon fancier with an arrow of blood pointing south, and on her belly the words: *This pussy is mine*" (217). This act of possession—or claiming of something that was not his—is similar to the husband's implied theft. It not only objectifies Olimpia, making her body a tool for his use, but it also has devastating consequences. "That same night, Olimpia Zuleta undressed in front of her husband, having forgotten what was scrawled there, and he did not say a word, his breathing did not even change, nothing, but he went to the bathroom for his razor while she was putting on her nightgown, and in a single slash he cut her throat" (217). Florentino never expresses or feels remorse over this horrific event. Instead, he worries about retribution from the husband and a public scandal that would reveal this affair to Fermina. Given the fact that Florentino is the romantic hero of the text, this callousness is startling. Yet it reflects the deception that he practices with women as well as the reader.

Perhaps, his most disturbing relationship is with América Vicuña, a school girl and "recognized blood relative. [. . .] She was still a child in every sense of the word, with braces on her teeth and the scrapes of elementary school on her knees" (272). The sixty-year age difference puts Nabokov's Humbert Humbert to shame, but both América and Lolita use sex to control an older man.[13] In the case of Florentino, América tries to win him back from Fermina:

[13] M. Keith Booker also discusses this connection with *Lolita* in "The Dangers of Gullible Reading: Narrative as Seduction in García Márquez's *Love in the Time of Cholera*." "Humbert Humbert is a pervert, a rapist, and a murderer, and we are reminded repeatedly in *Lolita* of his mental and physical cruelty. Yet he is also a master

Now she was a full-fledged woman, who liked to take the initiative. She continued typing with just one finger of her right hand, and with her left for his leg, explored him, found him, felt him come to life, grow, heard him sigh with excitement, and his old man's breathing became uneven and labored. She knew him: from that point on he was going to lose control, his speech would become disjointed, he would be at her mercy, and he would not find his way back until he had reached the end. (295–6)

Her control is fleeting, however. Not only is his passion for Fermina stronger (in the long run) than her seductive prowess, but he also views América as just another affair: "Florentino loved her as he had loved so many other casual women in his long life, but he loved her with more anguish than any other, because he was certain he would be dead by the time she finished secondary school" (274). Not surprisingly, when Urbino dies, Florentino abandons her in pursuit of Fermina, and remains oblivious to—or at least conveniently ignorant of—the pain he is causing her: "He never imagined how much she suffered during her sleepless nights at school, during the weekends without him, during her life without him, because he never imagined how much she loved him" (316). He cannot imagine these things because he is not invested in her emotionally or psychologically. He cannot imagine these things because his single-minded pursuit of Fermina blinds him to the feelings of others.

He also neglects América as a guardian, and like his treatment of Olimpia, this has devastating consequences. When América's grades

of language who constructs a narrative so charming and so brilliant that many readers are seduced into sympathy with his position and are able to accept his claims that his relationship with Lolita was purely aesthetic. Similarly, Ariza's numerous love stories (especially the central one involving Fermina) make such attractive narratives that we are tempted to read him as the ideal lover he apparently thinks himself to be, not as the manipulative womanizer who jumps from one bed to another, causing considerable suffering and multiple violent deaths among the objects of this insatiable sexual appetite. Indeed, like Nabokov, García Márquez sprinkles his text with reminders of the sinister side of Ariza's sexual exploits—and exploitation" (190).

at school begin plummeting, Florentino decides not to contact her parents and refuses to "discuss it with her because of a well-founded fear that she would try to implicate him in her failure. [. . .] Without realizing it, he was beginning to defer his problems in the hope that death would resolve them" (316). By ignoring her, he is both refusing to accept responsibility as her caretaker/lover and trying to assuage his guilt. This behavior is not only cowardly, but it reinforces the fact that he has simply used her for sex. His selfish silence and neglect ultimately devastates América, and she disappears from the text, as well as his life, for the next twenty pages.

When Florentino finally achieves his lifelong goal of being with Fermina, however, América kills herself, and García Márquez brings these moments together to undermine a romanticized reading of the end. During the cruise, Florentino receives an urgent telegram with a single line: *"América Vicuña dead yesterday reasons unknown"* (336). He immediately knows the reasons but tries to ignore them:

América Vicuña in the grip of mortal depression because she had failed her final examinations, had drunk a flask of laudanum stolen from the school infirmary. [. . . She] had left no explanatory note that would have allowed anyone to be blamed for her decision. [. . .] The only thing he could do to stay alive was not to allow himself the anguish of that memory. He erased it from his mind, although from time to time in the years that were left to him he would feel it revive, with no warning and for no reason, like the sudden pang of an old scar. (336)

Florentino's response is to "erase" it, like he tried erasing her after Urbino's death, but the guilt he has so skillfully evaded briefly catches up with him: "At a certain moment, the pangs of grief for América Vicuña made him twist with pain, and he could not hold off the truth any longer: he locked himself in the bathroom and cried, slowly, until his last tear was shed. Only then did he have the courage to admit to himself how much he had loved her" (346).

This is yet another deceptive moment. It is not love, but guilt that makes him cry in private. Despite these tears, there is no indication that this moment changes him. He does not tell América's parents or Fermina about the affair. He does not go to the funeral. As readers, we are left wondering if the love between Florentino and Fermina is something we should root for, if it is worth the sacrifices that have been made. From this perspective, the ambiguous ending may be less about finding a love that lasts "forever" than escaping the ramifications of such devastating choices.

Lastly, García Márquez reinforces this dichotomy between love and sex, as well as his critique of the romanticization of sex, by making the first sexual encounter between Fermina and Florentino ineffectual and hollow. On their first night together, Florentino is impotent: "Then she took the final step: she searched for him where he was not, she searched again without hope, and she found him, unarmed. 'It's dead,' he said [. . .] He was ashamed, furious with himself, longing for some reason to blame her for his failure" (340). Later that night, he returns with a kind of fury to her room, and has sex with her so quickly and forcefully that she feels hollow:

> His guard was up, and she realized that he did not expose his weapon by accident, but displayed it as if it were a war trophy in order to give himself courage. He did not even give her time to take off the nightgown that she had put on when the dawn breeze began to blow, and his beginner's haste made her shiver with compassion. But that did not disturb her, because in such cases it was not easy to distinguish between compassion and love. When it was over, however, she felt empty. (340)

Like many of Florentino's other lovers, she is moved more by compassion than love, and the war imagery in this description suggests that sex is not at about love, but conquest and self-satisfaction.

An Unending War

"There was no reason to complain, however, if the Europeans themselves were once again setting the bad example of a barbaric war when we had begun to live in peace after nine civil wars in half a century, which, if the truth were told, were all one war: always the same war" (191). This ominous, final phrase suggests that peace will always be fleeting in such a volatile nation. As discussed in the biographical section, political unrest and war have ravaged Colombia for over one-hundred-and-fifty years, and García Márquez typically incorporates the social ramifications of this in his fiction. Not surprisingly, political violence has a tangible, recurring presence in *Love in the Time of Cholera,* and much like the realities of cholera and modernization, war stands in contrast to the romanticization of love.

Dr. Urbino is neither romantic nor political, in part, because of his status as an aristocrat. In many ways, he considers himself above the messiness of passion and partisan politics. Early in the novel, he feels relieved to be at the age where sex is no longer a concern: "The only consolation, even for someone like him who had been a good man in bed, was sexual peace: the slow, merciful extinction of his venereal appetite" (40). For a man who needs to feel in control, sexual desire is a weakness and its gradual loss "merciful." Likewise, he does not want his actions and beliefs to be dictated by a political party: "In his opinion a Liberal president was exactly the same as a Conservative president, but not as well dressed. [. . .] He would have liked to point out to [the Archbishop] that guests were at the luncheon not because of what they thought but because of the merits of their lineage, which was something that had always stood over and above the hazards of politics and the horrors of war" (35). Clearly, Urbino believes that "the merits [. . .] of lineage" speak to a person's importance in society and that bloodline and a good family name elevate one above politics. Even the political parties recognize his indifference, considering such views archaic and undesirable:

> He defined himself as a natural pacifist, a partisan of definitive reconcili-ation between Liberals and Conservatives for the good of the nation. But his public conduct was so autonomous that no group claimed him for its own: the Liberals considered him a Gothic troglodyte, the Conservatives said that he was almost a Mason, and the Masons repudiated him as a secret cleric in the service of the Holy See. His less savage critics thought he was just an aristocrat enraptured by the delights of the Poetic Festival while the nation bled to death in an endless civil war. (44)

This passage suggests that Urbino's political indifference is irrespon-sible—especially given his status and power in the community. From the perspective of these groups, Urbino should be doing something more than passively hoping for party "reconciliation," but he chooses not to because politics is messy. By presenting Ur-bino in this way, García Márquez is not trying to promote the ac-tions of one party over the other; instead, he suggests that inaction is not a socially responsible solution when those around you suffer.

Like Urbino, Florentino is apolitical, and he disregards the reali-ties of war and cholera in order to preserve his romantic ideals. While on his first riverboat trip, Florentino witnesses the dangers of both firsthand. The journey—already made miserable by the op-pressive heat and voracious mosquitoes—is complicated by the cur-rent war: "Moreover, another episode of the intermittent civil war between Liberals and Conservatives had broken out that year, and the Captain had taken very strict precautions to maintain internal order and protect the safety of passengers" (141). These precautions include restrictions on shooting alligators from the deck (not to have the gunfire mistaken for military action) and on leaving the boat for fear of contagion. At one point, Florentino sees "three bloated, green, human corpses float past, with buzzards sitting on them. First the bodies of two men went by, one of them without a head, and then a very young girl, whose medusan locks undulated in the boat's wake. He never knew, because no one ever knew, if they were victims of the cholera or the war" (142). One of the passengers on the inaugural balloon journey expresses the same uncertainty: "The pilot, who was observing the world through the spyglass, said: 'They seem dead.' He passed the spyglass to Dr. Juvenal Urbino, who saw the oxcarts in the cultivated fields, the boundary lines of the railroad tracks, the blighted irrigation ditches, and wherever he looked he saw human bodies. Someone said that the cholera was ravaging the villages of the Great Swamp. Dr. Urbino, as he spoke, continued to look through the spyglass. 'Well, it must be a very special form of cholera,' he said, 'because every single corpse has received the coup de grace through the back of the neck'" (226–27). Even though Urbino implies that these are victims of war, not cholera, both cases remain unclear since people can be killed by or for having cholera as well as differing political beliefs. This conflation also suggests that both politics and cholera inspire violence—a violence so pervasive in this region that distinguishing its origin is almost impossible.

For Florentino, the horror of this moment is dulled by his first sexual encounter that same evening: "A hand like the talon of a hawk seized him by the shirt sleeve and pulled him into a cabin. In the darkness he could barely see the naked woman [. . .] who pushed him onto the bunk face up, unbuckled his belt, unbuttoned his trousers, impaled herself on him as if she were riding horseback, and stripped him, without glory, of his virginity. [. . .] Then she lay for a moment on top of him, gasping for breath, and she ceased to exist in the darkness. 'Now go and forget all about it,' she said. 'This never happened'" (142–43). After this "rape," which again equates love with violence, Florentino discovers that sex (without love) can be an escape from pain. He also realizes that "his illusory love for Fermina

Daza could be replaced by an earthly passion" (143). This is obviously not a romantic moment, but it is the starting point for his attitudes about love and sex. His obsession with Fermina and womanizing enable him to shut out the social realities of war and cholera. This disinterest is evident in his second riverboat trip at the end of the novel. He uses this voyage to escape the "real" world and live out his fantasy love with Fermina. He falsely raises the plague flag and blames the environmental deterioration on cities, not the riverboat company's exploitation of the land or the damaged caused by sickness and war. Like modernization, cholera, and even love, politics leads to violence. It destroys lives and landscapes. It makes aggression a mark of one's passion and commitment to something. And like so many relationships in the text, it disregards human casualties.

Aging

One of the innovations of this love story is García Márquez's focus on passion among the elderly. The ramifications of age on bodies, cities, rivers, governments, and, of course, love, preoccupy most of the characters in the text. For Urbino, Florentino, and Fermina, the passage of time makes them reconsider the things they have waited for—financial success, social status, personal happiness, professional recognition, and passion. In their attempts to preserve a sense of self (publicly and privately), they struggle not to view the aging body as a metaphor for loss. In fact, they use various means, including clothes, lotions, perfumes, travel, and sex, to mitigate the deterioration of their aging bodies—in effect, to appear attractive and capable to others.

Both Urbino and Florentino worry about the public perception of their aging bodies. Dr. Urbino specifically tries to hide the signs of age through clothing. On his eightieth birthday, he still wears "a linen suit, with a gold watch chain across his vest, as smartly as he had in his younger years" (4). Yet this elegant apparel is somewhat undermined by the fact that Fermina must dress him: "She could not remember when she had also begun to help him dress, and finally to dress him, and she was aware that at first she had done it for love, but for the past five years or so she had been obliged to do it regardless of the reason because he could not dress himself" (26). Urbino is not terribly concerned about his failings in private—the inability to dress himself and the "merciful extinction" of sexual desire—but he does fear public opinion. When the rain makes a shambles of Dr. Olivella's and Aminta Dechamps's silver anniversary luncheon, for example, Urbino has to be helped from his carriage to the house: "He had to accept the humiliation of being carried by Don Sancho's men under a yellow canvas canopy" (34). For a man who has defined himself by social status (as an aristocrat and eminent doctor), this public display of dependency feels humiliating. It is a painful reminder of both his physical and mental deterioration. In fact, his greatest fear is memory loss, and this makes him aware of his waning ability to practice medicine:

Until the age of fifty he had not been conscious of the size and weight and condition of his organs. Little by little, as he lay with his eyes closed after his daily siesta, he had begun to feel them, one by one, inside his body, feel the shape of his insomniac heart, his mysterious liver, his hermetic pancreas, and he had slowly discovered that even the oldest people were younger than he was and that he had become the only survivor of his generation's legendary group portraits. When he became aware of his first bouts of forgetfulness, he had recourse to a tactic he had heard about from one of his teachers at the Medical School: "The man who has no memory makes one out of paper." But this was a short-lived illusion, for he reached the stage where he would forget what the written reminders in his pockets meant [. . .]. But what disturbed him the most was his lack of confidence in his own power of reason: little by little, as in an ineluctable shipwreck, he felt himself losing his good judgment. (40)

He lists his organs as if he were discovering them for the first time, and in a sense, he is. Only after turning fifty does he begin to recognize his body as aged, as something made up of organs that will eventually fail. It is the failure of his memory, however, that terrifies him the most, for the extent of his forgetfulness signals the end of his medical career—the end of his public and private identity as a doctor.

Florentino is also terrified by aging and tries a variety of ways to mitigate its effects: "He was never as afraid of death as he was reaching that humiliating age when he would have to be led on a woman's arm. On that day, and only on that day, he knew he would have to renounce his hope of Fermina Daza" (257). For Florentino, dependency means the end of physical attractiveness, which is too much a part of his identity to imagine losing, so he uses clothing, among other things, to mask his aging body. He does not attempt to look too young, however, because that would be scoffed at publicly. "But no man of the time would have braved the ridicule of looking young at his age, even if he did or thought he did, and none would have dared to confess without shame that he still wept in secret over a rebuff received in the previous century. It was a bad time for being young: there was a style of dress for each age, but the style for old age began soon after adolescence, and lasted until the grave. More than age, it was a matter of social dignity" (260). Long before this trend, Florentino was dressing like an old man, and this uniformity gives him a somewhat ageless quality. "His body was bony and erect, his skin dark and clean-shaven, his eyes avid behind round spectacles in silver frames, and he wore a romantic old-fashioned mustache with waxed tips" (48). We also learn that he "spent a great deal of money, ingenuity, and will power to disguise the seventy-six years

he had completed in March" (48). Some of this money and ingenuity went toward numerous cures for hair loss. "His greatest battle,
fought tooth and nail and lost without glory, was against baldness"
(261). He "tried one hundred seventy two" cures, but none worked.
At a certain point, he "accepted his baldness with all his heart, he
attributed it to the masculine virtues that he had heard about and
scorned as nothing but the fantasies of bald men. Later he took refuge in the new custom of combing long hairs from his part on the
right all the way across his head, and this he never abandoned"
(262–63). As with so many things in Florentino's life, his battle
against baldness is fought in the hopes of remaining sexually attractive to women. But like his false teeth and broken ankle, hair loss
reminds him of his increasing frailty and age.

Florentino also uses clothing to feel virile and sexually desirous.
When he waits for Fermina on the *New Fidelity*, for example, he
wears an anachronistic outfit:

He looked different to her, not only because she saw him now with other
eyes, but because in reality he had changed. Instead of the funeral clothing
he had worn all his life, he was dressed in comfortable white shoes, slacks,
and a linen shirt with an open collar. [. . .] He also had on a white Scottish
cap and removable dark lenses over his perpetual eyeglasses for myopia. It
was evident that everything was being used for the first time and had been
bought just for the trip. [. . .] Seeing him like this, dressed just for her in so
patent a manner, she could not hold back the fiery blush that rose to her
face. (330–31)

The complete contrast (from a black to a white suit) is meant to star-
tle Fermina and deflect attention from his aging body. The open
shirt is youthful. The cap covers his ever-thinning hair. And the sunglasses hide his myopia. Even though Fermina recognizes this
change as part of a strategy to win her affections, she doesn't know
Florentino well enough to place this into a more problematic and

disturbing context. Like the notes sent via carrier pigeon to Olimpia (the pigeon fancier) and ice cream on Sundays with América, Florentino's appearance is a tool for seduction—a tool with dangerous consequences.

Before his renewed pursuit of Fermina, Florentino had also used sex (much like clothes and sunglasses) to resist the ravages of age. His preference for widows offers one example of this: "Florentino had come to realize that the world was full of happy widows. [. . .] So many widows in his life [. . .] had made it possible for him to discern how happy they were after the death of their husbands" (202–3). It is not merely their happiness that he finds surprising and reassuring, but the fact that they are older than he. For much of his life, Florentino tries to feel younger by loving older women, but this changes with América: "he loved her with more anguish than any other, because he was certain he would be dead by the time she finished secondary school" (275). Part of the intensity of this relationship (for Florentino) comes from his age. As discussed earlier in this chapter, his relationship with a pre-teen girl (and relative) is repulsive, but it can also be understood in the context of his anxieties about aging, dependency, and death. Sex with her makes him feel like a desirable lover, and he needs to hold onto this identity in order to court Fermina.

Like Urbino, Fermina responds to age, as well as love, in accordance with her social status. As an aristocrat, she sees herself as above the pitfalls of age, and this is evident in her shock at Cousin Hildebranda's appearance after a prolonged separation: "When she saw her waiting at the door she almost fainted: it was as if she were seeing herself in the mirror of truth. She was fat and old, burdened with unruly children [. . .]. But she was still the same person inside her ruined body. Fermina Daza recovered from the shock after just a few days of country living and pleasant memories" (253). Fermina needs to see herself as the same person because of her position in society. Despite her "ruined body," she still carries herself with elegance and dignity until her reputation is tarnished by two articles in the tabloids. At this moment, she ages rapidly: "But one or the other, or both, had annihilated her. Her hair, the color of stainless steel, had ennobled her face, but now it looked like ragged yellow strands of corn silk, and her beautiful panther eyes did not recover their old sparkle even in the brilliant heat of her anger. Her decision not to go on living was evident in every gesture" (321). By linking her physical deterioration with this scandal, García Márquez reinforces the ways in which she has learned to define herself by class. Her body is clearly linked with a sense of social importance.

Fermina is not merely anxious about the public perception of her body, but also about the ways in which her body will be viewed in private, intimate spaces. When Florentino first tries to kiss her during their cruise, she stops him. He "pressed her hand, bent toward her, and tried to kiss her on the cheek. But she refused, in her hoarse, soft voice. 'Not now,' she said to him, 'I smell like an old woman'" (329). Later, he understands what she means: "Florentino Ariza shuddered: as she herself had said, she had the sour smell of old age. [. . .] He consoled himself with the thought that he must give off the same odor [. . .]. It was the smell of human fermentation, which he had perceived in his oldest lovers and they had detected in him" (335). Fermina shows an awareness about her aging body that has never occurred to Florentino. Even after she freshens up, for example, she worries that Florentino may not find her attractive. She even asks him not to look at her body when they first try to have sex: "'Because you won't like it.' [. . .] Her shoulders were wrinkled, her breasts sagged, her ribs were covered by a flabby skin as pale and cold as a frog's. She covered her chest with the blouse she had just taken off, and she turned out the light" (339). She clearly accepts aging more honestly, and with more resignation, than Florentino. But despite moments of defensiveness (such as throwing her daugh-

ter out of the house for insulting her relationship with Florentino),
Fermina comes to terms with her anxieties about aging in ways that
the men in the novel never do.

Color Lines

For most of the characters in *Love in the Time of Cholera*, racism
limits the possibilities for love. It is not only evident in various social
structures and communal attitudes, but also in the ways that sexual
desire for the racial "other" is interpreted. Blacks and the poor are
essentially ghettoized in the old slave quarters. The "good" and
"bad" Chinese, who work in restaurants and laundries, are often
mistrusted (194). Overall, the town is so rooted in racial hierarchies
that interracial relationships seem unthinkable. There are two minor
exceptions. Florentino, who has a fluid social status, doesn't seem to
share these biases, in part, because he sees all women, regardless of
ethnicity, class, occupation, and physical appearance, as objects of
sexual desire: "He picked up serving girls in the parks, black women
in the market, sophisticated young ladies from the interior on the
beaches, gringas on the boats from New Orleans" (175). Second,
Jeremiah de Saint-Amour, whose disability relegates him to his
apartment and marginalizes him from the community, has a relationship with a black woman that is arguably one of the most loving
in the novel. "She had been with him for half his life, with a devotion and submissive tenderness that bore too close a resemblance to
love. [. . .] She cleaned and straightened the laboratory once a week,
but not even the most evil-minded neighbors confused appearance
with reality because they, like everyone else, supposed that Jeremiah
de Saint-Amour's disability affected more than his capacity to walk"
(13–14). Urbino cannot imagine a love that crosses ethnic lines, yet
her devotion to Jeremiah rivals Florentino's love for Fermina. Jere-

miah "had made the irrevocable decision to take his own life when he was sixty years old" (15), and by helping him die, she makes the ultimate sacrifice out of respect for his wishes. Nevertheless, like her status in the community, she remains nameless in the text, and in this way, García Márquez focuses our attention on the racial prejudices that make such a relationship taboo.

García Márquez specifically uses Urbino's and Fermina's racism—once again—to undermine a romanticized reading of these figures and the text. Urbino is shocked, for example, about both Jeremiah's affair and his lover's response to it: "a clandestine life shared with a man who was never completely hers, and in which they often knew the sudden explosion of happiness, did not seem to her a condition to be despised. On the contrary: life had shown her that perhaps it was exemplary" (14). Urbino views this relationship as illicit because of her race and because he had always viewed his own liaison with a black woman in those terms. This racism is also evident in his description of the old slave quarters: "Everything looked wretched and desolate, but out of the sordid taverns came the thunder of riotous music, the godless drunken celebration of Pentecost by the poor. [. . .] The exterior of the unnumbered house was in no way distinguishable from its less fortunate neighbors, except for the window with lace curtains and an imposing front door take from some old church" (13). Most of these descriptions rely on stereotypes ("riotous music" and "godless drunken celebration"), and by implication, he is blaming their poverty on this behavior, not larger social conditions. Like this woman who remains nameless to him, Urbino refers to her house as indistinguishable from all the rest, suggesting his attitude about the poor more broadly—that they are all the same.

Urbino later has an affair with a black woman but cannot escape his own prejudices to love her. He met Miss Barbara Lynch at the clinic of Misericordia Hospital, and "he knew immediately that something irreparable had just occurred in his destiny. She was a tall, elegant, large-boned mulatta, with skin the color and softness of molasses. [. . .] Her sex seemed more pronounced than that of other human beings" (241). He initially sees her in stereotypical terms— with dark skin like molasses, exotic clothes, and possessing a hypersexuality. His desire becomes so consuming that he jeopardizes his professional integrity by using a routine exam as an excuse to fondle her: "Then he gave himself over to the delights of touch, no longer the best-qualified physician along the Caribbean coastline but a poor soul tormented by his tumultuous instincts" (243). Though he immediately admits his attraction to her, she would not let him disrobe her: "Black I am but not a fool" (243). She recognizes the power disparity not merely because of his class and social status, but also because of her race. Barbara Lynch is anything but a stereotype (she is a Doctor of Theology, the daughter of a Reverend, and a woman who carries herself with sophistication, elegance, and a good command of languages), yet Urbino only sees her as a sexual object:

> Without time to say anything, Miss Lynch would go to the bedroom as soon as she saw her agitated lover walk in the door. [. . .] But he squandered everything she did to make him happy. Panting and drenched with perspiration, he rushed after her into the bedroom [. . .] and made panic-stricken love with his trousers around his knees, with his jacket buttoned so that it would not get in his way [. . .]. She was left dangling, barely at the entrance of her tunnel of solitude, while he was already buttoning up again, as exhausted as if he had made absolute love on the dividing line between life and death, when in reality he had accomplished no more than the physical act that is only a part of the feat of love. (246)

She is described as both unsatisfied and arguably more isolated than before she knew him. Urbino's fear of being caught intensifies with each visit, and he can only find solace when he decides to confess, end the affair, and try to return to his marriage and life of privilege.

He reneges his promises and treats her without compassion or respect: "The vows of eternal love, the dream of a discreet house for her along [. . .] everything he had promised in the blazing heat of love was canceled forever after. [. . .] Dr. Urbino never saw her again, not even by accident, and God alone knows how much grief his heroic resolve cost him or how many bitter tears he had to shed behind the locked lavatory door in order to survive this private catastrophe" (248). Even in this description, we only get access to his pain, not to Barbara's sense of abandonment and betrayal. Urbino's callousness stems from both the impropriety of such an affair (an aristocrat with a black woman) and the loss of his marriage (which would tarnish his public appearance).

Fermina's response to ethnicity and race is also informed by their class and social status. Fermina admits that she would have never expected an affair with Barbara Lynch because of her race (and by extension, class). While going through one of Urbino's notebooks, she noticed her entry: "The name attracted her attention, and it suddenly occurred to her that she was one of those dissolute artists from the New Orleans fruit boats, but the address made her think that she must come from Jamaica, a black woman, of course, and she eliminated her without a second thought as not being to her husband's taste" (242). Her ambiguity here is more a symptom of her class than her true feelings. She assumes that her husband would not have an affair with a black women. In fact, she says this explicitly after Urbino confesses: "'And worst of all, damn it: with a black woman.' He corrected her: 'With a mulatta.' But by then it was too late for accuracy: she had finished. 'Just as bad,' she said, 'and only now I understand: it was the smell of a black woman'" (250). Like Fermina's outrage over the fact that Urbino confessed to a priest, she detests the thought of his affair with a black woman. Again, the pubic implications of such an affair make her feel humiliated and ashamed. Her aristocratic status exposes her latent prejudices.

García Márquez continually undermines our desire to read *Love in the Time of Cholera* as a romance, a magical love story with a happy ending. Issues of class, modernity, illness, sexual desire, violence, age, and ethnicity complicate lives and relationships. This text uses these—as well as other elements—to challenge socially-constructed idealizations of love. Love is many things in this novel. It involves compassion, compromise, tenderness, desire, anger, longing, sex, pain, suffering, and satisfaction. As this list suggests, love is always more complex than it first appears. People are often manipulated and deceived by the rhetoric and clichéd behaviors of love. And ultimately, the novel plays with our own desires for, and idealizations of, love. It lures us with a poetry, beauty, and longing that we all share.

3

The Novel's Reception

With the publication of *Love in the Time of Cholera*, Gabriel García Márquez once again beguiled readers with his elegant prose and beautifully complex explorations of love. Author Thomas Pynchon even sighed in admiration: "Oh boy—does he write well. He writes with impassioned control, out of a maniacal serenity."[14] While most reviews praise the language of the novel, they also note García Márquez's ability to craft fiction that both resonates with his earlier work and stands apart from it. Pynchon describes *Love* as a journey that takes us "a meaningful distance from Macondo, the magical village in *One Hundred Years of Solitude*."[15] And reviewer Robert Couteau considers it a stylistic achievement: "While *Love in the Time of Cholera* has formal similarities to his other great fictional works—*One Hundred Years of Solitude* and *The Autumn of the Patriarch*—it avoids an exclusive reliance on either the stunning halluci-

---

[14] See "The Heart's Eternal Vow," *New York Times Book Review* (April 10, 1988), pp. 1, 47, 49. Reprinted on: www.themodernword.com/pynchon/pynchon_essays_cholera.html.

[15] Ibid.

natory quality of the former or the lush density of the latter."[16] It is García Márquez's innovation—what David Castronovo calls "amazing versatility and range"[17]—that reviewers highlight as the singular achievement of the text. It also evinces García Márquez's fearless ability to move in new directions without being haunted by the tremendous success of *One Hundred Years of Solitude*.

Pynchon's insightful review, "The Heart's Eternal Vow" (*New York Times*, April 10, 1988), begins by describing Márquez's subject matter—love—as revolutionary: "In the postromantic ebb of the 70s and 80s, with everybody now so wised up and even growing paranoid about love, once the magical buzzword of a generation, it is a daring step for any writer to decide to work in love's vernacular, to take it, with all its folly, imprecision and lapses in taste, at all seriously." Indeed, García Márquez embraces both the sentimental excesses and the genuine power of love. With Florentino, a character who follows through on his pledge to love someone "forever," García Márquez suggests that these versions of passion can coexist simultaneously—and often do in most of us. After a fifty-year wait, Florentino may be racing against the clock to win Fermina's love, but the passing of time only intensifies his desire. For Pynchon, this portrayal of love and time "is revolutionary in daring to suggest that vows of love made under a presumption of immortality—youthful idiocy, to some—may yet be honored, much later in life when we ought to know better, in the face of the undeniable."

We may know better. We may be skeptical of Florentino's clichéd declarations and outrageous tactics. But García Márquez makes us

---

[16] See Robert Couteau "Love in the Time of Cholera," *Arete Magazine* (December 1988). Reprinted on his website: http://members.tripod.com/more_couteau/marquez.htm.

[17] See David Castronovo "Love in the Time of Cholera," *America* (September 10, 1988), p. 146.

root for him in spite of ourselves. We are torn between our support for Florentino, "wishing for the success of this stubborn warrior against age and death [. . .] in the name of love," and his flaws. This tension, Pynchon argues, is central to our relationship with the text. We cheer for Florentino because we accept him as human—as someone with faults, passions, charms, and missteps. And Pynchon believes that this accounts for our willingness to forgive his "dangerous indifference to consequences that often borders on criminal neglect." Perhaps, we are forgiving because so many other characters—women in particular—forgive and love him. In fact, Florentino only survives because of the support of women, namely his mother, Leona Cassiani, and even América. As Pynchon states, women in Márquez's fiction are typically "stronger, more attuned to reality" than men. Walter Clemmons's review in *Newsweek* ("The Sweet Plague of Love," April 25, 1988) reinforces this reading, noting the significant roles that strong women play in the text: "Fermina Daza is an unusual heroine, sturdy, bad-tempered and not always likable."[18] Like all of the main characters in *Love*, Fermina is complicated. She is both likable and frustrating, tender and cruel. García Márquez uses this multifaceted portrait (as well as details such as her passion for smoking) to keep this love story from becoming sentimental despite all of its clichés. As Clemmons reminds us, García Márquez has always considered himself a social realist: "'I've always been convinced that my true profession is that of a journalist,' he once told Peter H. Stone in *The Paris Review*."[19] Even when García Márquez's realism is infused with the fantastic, he never neglects to show the ways in which human experience and feeling are affected by social realities such as war, disease, political corruption, and mortality.

[18] Walter Clemmons, "The Sweet Plague of Love," *Newsweek* (April 25, 1988), p. 61.

[19] Ibid., p. 60.

Pynchon concludes his review from the standpoint of a writer, claiming that the only honest way to write about love is for an author "to control his own love for his characters, to withhold the full extent of his caring, in other words not to lapse into drivel." García Márquez does this admirably. He may play with a range of romantic genres—sentimental novel, soap opera, erotica—but he never loses sight of what is profound and moving about Florentino and Fermina's love. The integrity of this vision leaves us with what Pynchon calls a "shining and heartbreaking novel."

Robert Couteau's review in *Arete Magazine* (December 1988) also focuses on some of the tensions surrounding love in the novel: "Maintaining an almost folktale quality grounded with the feel of everyday gossip, it incorporates images of love which hover midway between otherworldly beauty and netherworld terror." This terror comes, in part, from the compromises that Fermina and Urbino make in order to get married. Their union is one of social and personal convenience. Urbino wants an elegant, beautiful wife to reinforce his aristocratic status. Fermina wants the kind of financial security and social position that Urbino can offer. Couteau finds this exploration of convenience one of the most powerful aspects of the novel. Since their marriage is "successful" in many ways, García Márquez uses this tension to ask us to examine the compromises we ourselves make for love.

Terror also resides in the more ugly and hurtful aspects of love. "All the meaningless forays of everyday life shared by two people thus bond together—all the rather unpleasant smells, degrading tasks and dulling routines; all the unspoken bitterness and rancor; all the sullen weight of unlived possibilities—are here unmercifully catalogued."[20] Yet García Márquez offers some balance to this por-

---

[20] Robert Couteau, "Love in the Time of Cholera." http://members.tripod.com/more_couteau/marquez.htm

trait. Despite these disturbing moments, love still exists and grows in these places. As Couteau states, love not only has the power to transcend these "dark interstices," but it can also transform nostalgia into reality. Ultimately, it is Florentino's gradual, and rather reluctant, acceptance of reality that enables him to love Fermina realistically.

Even reviews that misread the novel tend to praise it highly. In "The Novel as Tropical Flower" (*Economist*, July 2, 1988), for example, the reviewer begins by foregrounding the magical elements of the text:

Mr. García Márquez plays around a little with time, sometimes leaping backwards or forwards without warning; and the world he describes has the quality of dreams. Characters act without apparent motivation; perfumed crows are kept on the balconies of respectable houses; a man dressed in black, with a stovepipe hat, goes out in a boat to salvage treasure from a galleon that does not exist; the heroine tosses bottles of cough syrup out of a balloon. When all this is said, however, what remains is a classic novel in the old style.[21]

In many ways, this passage misrepresents the focus of the novel. It suggest that *Love in the Time of Cholera* is another example of García Márquez's use of magic realism (*à la One Hundred Years of Solitude*). Yet, as discussed earlier, these dream-like elements are a secondary, even marginal part of the text.

The reviewer also implies that these magical qualities are potentially problematic for readers (though they wouldn't surprise anyone familiar with García Márquez's works): "When all this is said, however, what remains is a classic novel in the old style." In other words, this "classic, [. . .] old style" somehow mitigates such fanciful mo-

---

[21] See "The Novel as Tropical Flower," *The Economist* (July 2, 1988), p. 77.

ments. The ambiguity of this phrase "old style" is never clarified or explained, but it seems to praise García Márquez for reverting back to nineteenth-century literary forms without recognizing the ways in which García Márquez parodies and satirizes such forms. The reviewer even accepts some of Florentino's declarations without question: "In his feckless womanizing, Florentino Ariza 'always behaved as if he were the eternal husband of Fermina Daza . . . who fought endlessly to free himself from servitude.'"[22] From reading the novel, we know that even Fermina doesn't believe such a statement. Despite these missteps, however, this reviewer does recognize the sensitivity and beauty that García Márquez brings to this exploration of love.

S. M. J. Minta's review in the *Times Literary Supplement* ("In Praise of the Popular," July 1–8, 1988) offers an effective counter to this misreading:

> Florentino can say "there is no greater glory than to die for love," and he can tell Fermina, after his thousand and one nights of infidelity, "I kept my virginity for you." And we shake our heads in disbelief. But the triumph of the novel is that it uncovers the massive, submerged strength of the popular, the clichéd and the sentimental, while the too solid world of Urbino, so reasonable, so lucid, so commendably progressive, is a world that is dying with him.[23]

Like Pynchon's and Couteau's reviews, this piece highlights García Márquez's ability to balance the everyday trials of love with the power of "the clichéd and sentimental." It is this tension that gives the text its humor and irony. It keeps it from slipping into the soap-opera clichés that it parodies.

[22] Ibid., p. 78.
[23] S. M. J. Minta "In Praise of the Popular," *Times Literary Supplement* (July 1–8, 1988), p. 730.

Perhaps the most problematic misreading by the reviewer of *The Economist* involves geography. He interprets the world of the novel as "virtually European. It is set in rooms, courtyards, streets, and offices. Fermina Daza dreams of Paris; Dr. Juvenal Urbino instructs the city in the sanitation and cares of Europe. The cultured folk of the city struggle for their opera and string quartets amid the chaos of epidemic and civil war."

This view could have been written by Urbino himself, for it only accounts for his perspective—or that of the local aristocracy. With the nagging presence of cholera, civil war, the old slave district, and the jungles surrounding the river, *Love in the Time of Cholera* is very much *about* Colombia. Once again, as the *Times Literary Supplement* states:

> It is a novel about commitment and fidelity under circumstances which seem to render such virtues absurd, about a refusal to grow old gracefully and respectably, about the triumph sentiment can still win over reason, and above all, perhaps, about Latin America, about keeping faith with where, for better or worse, you started out from.[24]

Urbino continually struggles with the stagnancy of "his" city in relation to European "progress." He also recognizes that the townspeople don't accept him as one of them. Likewise, Fermina struggles with her social and class status. She may dream of Paris, but not in the same way that she dreams of home. During her separation from Urbino, for example, she actually returns home to find comfort and solace. But she is disappointed by the vast changes; in part, because they reveal how much she has changed, how much she has lost contact with her roots. The town may remain unnamed—to give it a certain universality—but it is still very much situated in Colombia.

[24] Ibid.

Its political struggles, myths, people, racial divisions, and social dynamics cannot be understood apart from this setting.

Minta closes his review by considering a contemporary collection of essays, *Gabriel García Márquez: New Readings:*

The introduction points out that a conscious attempt has been made to present García Márquez's work through a broad range of critical perspectives, involving "practical criticism, thematic, formalist-structuralist, anthropological, psychoanalytical, Marxist, philosophy of language and deconstructionist readings." After the exhilaration of the new novel, a good deal of this feels inevitable, like heavy going, and sometimes García Márquez's texts stand uncomfortably in the way of a carnivorous erudition. Nevertheless, almost all of the essays in the collection can be consulted with profit.[25]

One of the challenges of academic criticism is situating a work in critical, social, and historical contexts. Unlike a book or film reviewer, whose opinions do not need to be grounded in any scholarly or intellectual discourse, a literary critic must balance innovative readings with research. In doing so, s/he participates in an ongoing dialogue about the text and author. Though Minta concedes that this collection has value, his critique of academic scholarship prevents him from highlighting other important aspects about *Love.* He suggests that the novel resists many of the critical frameworks imposed on it: "García Márquez's texts stand uncomfortably in the way of a carnivorous erudition."

On one level, this contention further compliments the text, suggesting that such a rich and multifaceted work cannot be reduced to a particular critical bent. But effective criticism does not impose a

---

[25] Ibid.

totalizing ideology. It does not demand that we read or interpret something from only one perspective. Whether using Marxist, feminist, or postcolonial perspectives, such readings merely open up new ways of looking at literature. And in the case of García Márquez, we can only benefit from learning more about the history of cholera and political strife in Colombia, for example.

In both reviews and academic criticism, writers ultimately praise García Márquez for the vision he shares with us. Like Florentino Ariza and Fermina Daza, we too take a riverboat journey—through love, passion, pain, politics, disease, death, and magic.

4

The Novel's Performance

In terms of popular appeal, Gabriel García Márquez's works perform spectacularly. The worldwide Spanish edition of *Love in the Time of Cholera*, for example, sold over a million copies. Five hundred thousand were purchased in Germany, and it remained on the bestseller list in France for twenty-two weeks. In the United States, the hardback edition alone sold nearly four-hundred-thousand copies. In part, this success can be attributed to García Márquez's sophisticated and beautifully-crafted prose. Like Mozart's music, which sounds deceptively simple on the surface, García Márquez's fiction is layered with a rich complexity that enables audiences to discover something new with each reading.

Biographer Bell-Villada compares this popular appeal to Victorian writers such as Charles Dickens and Victor Hugo: "In this regard García Márquez stands in the tradition of the nineteenth-century novelists, whose high art combined the common touch and thus enabled them to speak to large audiences, and who, in the notable case of Hugo, by representing a progressive and humane politics, could inspire genuine affection among their millions of devotees and serve as a positive example to them" (203). In much the same way, the art and politics of García Márquez have not only inspired genuine affection among his fans, but they have also contributed to his influence on contemporary writers as well as his status as an international celebrity.

Literary Performances

With the publication of *One Hundred Years of Solitude*, García Márquez began participating in, and influencing, literary postmodernism. Critic Brian McHale defines postmodernist fiction in terms of the questions driving these works: "Which world is this? What is to be done in it? Which of my selves is to do it? What kinds of worlds are there? How do they differ? What happens when the boundaries between worlds are violated?" In other words, postmodern fiction tends to question notions of truth and reality by bringing worlds together—such as the past and present, the mystical and the real.

Thomas Pynchon's award-winning novel *V.* (1961), for example, plays with traditional literary conventions to question our assumptions about history, knowledge, and reality. Like García Márquez's *Chronicle of a Death Foretold*, *V.* (in a way similar to that of Pynchon's *The Crying of Lot 49*) parodies detective fiction through Herbert Stencil's endless quest to discover the identity of Lady V. This novel, like *One Hundred Years of Solitude*, incorporates multiple perspectives about events and people and, as a result, presents readers with many levels of "reality." Like so much of García Márquez's fiction, *V.* asks us to recognize that a story, like history itself, cannot be understood apart from the person telling it.

John Barth also engages with similar questions about the nature of storytelling in *Chimera* (1972). This collection of three novellas retells the legends of Scheherazade, Perseus, and Bellerophon by intersecting them with present-day characters. In the first story "Dunyazadiad," Barth brings a version of himself—whom he describes as a struggling, middle-aged writer with writer's block—into the narrative with Scheherazade and her sister. He proceeds to tell them stories from *A Thousand and One Nights*, which Scheherazade then narrates to Shahryar to save her life. Again, this collision of worlds, particularly the intersection of past and present, is one of the defining features of postmodernist fiction and is a staple in much of García Márquez's writing. In fact, Barth not only viewed the work of Jorge Luis Borges as a model for contemporary fiction in the late 1960s, but by the 1980s, he cited *One Hundred Years of Solitude* as a model for postmodern fiction, praising it as a "synthesis of straightforwardness and artifice, realism and magic and myth, political passion and nonpolitical artistry, characterization and caricature, humor and terror."[26] Ultimately, Barth concludes that García Márquez's skill as a storyteller not only makes his fiction "wonderful" and "important," but it also transcends the bounds of literary movements.

More recently, one can see similarities between García Márquez and Toni Morrison's use of folk culture and the supernatural. In *Beloved*, for example, the characters cannot escape their traumatic experiences with and memories of slavery. The past not only haunts the protagonist, Sethe, psychologically and emotionally, but it is also manifested in the literal return of Beloved—Sethe's dead daughter, whom she killed to keep from being enslaved. Like García Márquez, Morrison uses the fantastic (particularly the relationship between the living and dead) to examine the social ramifications of violence and history in her fiction.

Many literary critics have also discussed the influence of García Márquez on the works of British writer Jeanette Winterson. Several of her novels, such as *The Passion* (1987), *Sexing the Cherry* (1989), *Art and Lies* (1994), and *Gut Symmetries* (1997), share García Már-

[26] Quoted in Bell Villada's *García Márquez: The Man and His Work*, p. 207.

quez's interest in telling love stories infused with magic and history. Both *Sexing the Cherry* and *The Passion* weave fairy tales with the main characters' quest for love. Jordan from *Sexing the Cherry*, for example, encounters a city in which "the entire population had been wiped out by love three times in a row" (80). He also learns of a church built with ice and a weightless city where people "spend their lives suspended" (108), living in homes without floors.

Like Barth's *Chimera*, *Sexing the Cherry* also meditates on the nature of time, forcing the present-day world to collide with the past and future: "The future and the present and the past exist only in our minds, and from a distance the borders of each shrink and fade like the borders of hostile countries seen from a floating city in the sky. The river runs from one country to another without stopping" (166).

Similarly in *The Passion*, Villanelle, whose webbed feet link her to the boatmen of Venice and enable her to walk across the city's canals, takes a journey to reclaim her heart from the Queen of Spades (who has it stored in a round indigo jar). Magic permeates every aspect of this novel, and Winterson uses this magic to question the nature of storytelling and truth. As Henri reminds us at the end of the novel: "I'm telling you stories. Trust me" (160). In many respects, these magical and painfully real stories of love pay homage to the vision of García Márquez.

Online Performances

García Márquez's immense popularity has made him a celebrity and, as a result, the subject of much discussion on the internet. Early in the summer of 1999, García Márquez felt fatigued and decided to check himself into a hospital. Almost immediately, rumors began circulating in cyberspace about his failing health. Each speculation—exhaustion, a nervous breakdown, leukemia—became increasingly dire, and on July 9th, someone pretending to represent a wire agency claimed that García Márquez had died the previous evening.

Though doctors eventually determined that García Márquez had lymphatic cancer, this news wasn't released to the public for several months. He started receiving treatment, and from all accounts, he has improved. But persistent rumors still describe his health as declining, and in many respects, these stories mythologize the man himself.

About a year later, another hoax appeared. On May 29, 2000, the Peruvian newspaper *La República* published what they called García Márquez's "farewell poem"—a piece supposedly sent to close friends in response to his rapid deterioration. This poem, entitled "The Puppet," was reprinted the following day in a Mexico City paper, *La Crónica*, and subsequently spread like a wildfire on the internet. Shortly afterward, the actual author of the poem corrected the rumors. According to the website http://www.museumofhoaxes .com/marquez.html, "the poem turned out to be the work of an obscure Mexican ventriloquist named Johnny Welch. Welch had written the poem for his puppet sidekick 'Mofles,' but somehow his name had been replaced by the name of the Nobel Prize winning author." The ironic humor of the actual source (a ventriloquist) and the context (a poem for a puppet named Mofles) goes without saying. Yet on a superficial level, some of its themes resonate with works like *Love in the Time of Cholera*—as this excerpt from the poem suggests:

I would prove to the men how mistaken they are in thinking that they no longer fall in love when they grow old—not knowing that they grow old when they stop falling in love. To a child I would give wings, but I would let him learn how to fly by himself. To the old I would teach that death comes not with old age but with forgetting. I have learned so much from you men. . . .

[. . .]

I have learned that a man only has the right to look down on another man when it is to help him to stand up. I have learned so many things from you, but in the end most of it will be no use because when they put me inside that suitcase, unfortunately I will be dying.

Certainly, the opening line recalls *Love in the Time of Cholera*, but its clichés and highly sentimental language would never appear in García Márquez's writing. Nevertheless, this work affected many readers. Even Mrinal Sen, an Indian filmmaker and friend of García Márquez, "told the *Hindustan Times* that upon reading the poem he was flooded with memories from his twenty years of acquaintance with the author." This type of response, however, can be seen as yet another testament to the widespread admiration and affection felt for Márquez.

Cinematic Performances

García Márquez has been interested in film throughout his career. While working for *El Spectador* in the early 1950s, he read film biography extensively and became "the first-ever regular film critic in Colombia."[27] He even studied film briefly in Rome while covering a story about Pope Pius XII. In 1961, after taking a bus tour of the American South with his wife and first son, Márquez settled in Mexico City with the intention of writing screenplays. For the next two years, he wrote over a dozen film scripts—some in collaboration with Carlos Fuentes—but these melodramatic works lacked the art-

[27] Ibid., p. 50.

istry and sophistication of his fiction. A few of his original screen-plays, however, have been made into small-scale films, namely *Juego peligroso* [A Dangerous Game] (1966), *Tiempo de morir* [A Time to Die] (1985), and *Fábula de la Bella Palomera* [The Fable of the Beautiful Pigeon Fancier] (1988). Likewise, a number of his literary works have also been adapted for film, such as *Eréndira* (1983), *Chronicle of a Death Foretold* (1987), and *No One Writes to the Colonel* (1999). The last named, his most recent adaptation, premiered at the Cannes Film Festival in 1999 and was directed by famed Mexican director Arturo Ripstein. According to the website Gabriel García Márquez: Macondo http://www.themodernword.com/gabo, actor Antonio Banderas has expressed interest in directing a television series based on six unpublished stories by Márquez.

Whether in the world of literature, film, or cyberspace, Márquez's works continue to perform. They have influenced writers, touched fans, and inspired filmmakers. And just as *Love in the Time of Cholera* mythologizes and fictionalizes some of García Márquez's own experiences, his fans throughout the world have mythologized the man himself.

5

Further Reading and Discussion Questions

(1) After the tremendous international success and influence of *One Hundred Years of Solitude*, many readers expected García Márquez to write with a similar flair for the fantastic and exaggerated. The magical elements of this novel, such as a levitating priest, flying carpets, a young woman who rises to heaven while hanging her laundry, a trickle of blood that travels across town, and a rain of yellow flowers, still captivate readers. But this style of storytelling seems mostly absent from *Love in the Time of Cholera*. Why do you think García Márquez chose to present this story more realistically? Wouldn't Florentino fit comfortably into a narrative colored with the magical and extraordinary? Why does García Márquez use some of the realistic elements of the text (disease, aging, suffering) to undermine Florentino's penchant for idealization and exaggeration?

(2) García Márquez prefers to think of himself as a "realist" writer. As biographer Gene H. Bell-Villada explains, "'reality' for García Márquez consists not only of everyday events and economic hardships but also of such things as popular myths, beliefs, and home remedies—not just 'the facts' but what ordinary people say or think about the facts" (12). What do you make of the more hyper-

bolic moments in *Love in the Time of Cholera*—such as Florentino's 622 affairs and his visit to Olimpia Zuleta's grave?:

> Florentino buried her in the former Hand of God ranch, which was still known as the Cholera Cemetery, and he planted a rose bush on her grave. [. . .] When the roses bloomed he would place a flower on her grave if there was no one in sight, and later planted a cutting taken from his mother's rosebush. Both bloomed in such profusion that Florentino Ariza had to bring shears and other garden tools to keep them under control. But the task was beyond him: after a few years, the two rosebushes had spread like weeds among the graves, and from then on, the unadorned cemetery of the plague was called the Cemetery of Roses. (217–18)

Why incorporate this magical element here (at the grave of a woman whose death can be attributed to Florentino's actions)?

(3) Since *Love in the Time of Cholera* was inspired, in part, by the courtship and marriage of García Márquez's parents, several critics have viewed the similarities between their relationship and the characters' as an affirmation of marriage in general. Robin Fiddian, however, argues that the novel is an indictment of this institution. She cites several moments in which Fermina and Juvenal's relationship is described as a kind of "sterile captivity" and "servitude." Do you agree with her assessment of García Márquez's depiction of marriage? Why or why not?

(4) After Florentino hires Leona Cassiani to work for the Riverboat Company, their subsequent friendship becomes one of the most important relationships in his life. In fact, the narrator describes her as the only "true woman in his life although neither of them ever knew it and they never made love" (182). Leona's dedication to Florentino enables his rise in the company. "Her only objective was to clear the ladder at any cost, with blood if necessary, so that Florentino Ariza could move up to the position he had proposed for himself without calculating his own strength very well" (186). In

a novel so singularly focused on passion and romantic relationships, why does García Márquez create this relationship? What other moments in the text privilege platonic relationships over sexual relationships?

(5) Immediately after Juvenal's death, Florentino tells Fermina: "'I have waited for this opportunity for more than half a century, to repeat to you once again my vow of eternal fidelity and everlasting love" (50). This statement is as much about time as it is about love. How does the passage of time work for and against love? Consider the ways in which Fermina compares her youthful courtship with Florentino to his renewed efforts fifty years later. Why does Florentino prefer older women? Critic Manuel Martinez-Maldonado concludes that "although time defines human life [in *Love in the Time of Cholera*], ultimately love controls it" (129). Do you agree with this statement?

(6) M. Keith Booker discusses some of the challenges of García Márquez's seductive prose. "García Márquez demonstrates in *Love* that a well-told story can make readers accept almost anything. [. . . He constructs] a story that most readers will *want* to read in a positive way, due to the undeniable affirmation of humanity contained in readings of the book that emphasize the romance of the Ariza-Daza relationship" (191). What elements of the novel contribute to our desire to read this love story positively? What aspects undermine this reading?

(7) Violence permeates almost every aspect of the novel. War and cholera litter the landscape with dead bodies. Men murder women for infidelity. And sex is often motivated by either a loss of control or a need for power. García Márquez actually frames Florentino's story with moments of sexual violence. His first sexual experience is described as a kind of rape: "[She] pushed him onto the bunk face up, unbuckled his belt, unbuttoned his trousers, impaled herself on him as if she were riding horseback, and stripped him, without glory, of

his virginity" (142). Likewise, in the closing pages, Florentino consummates his relationship with Fermina in an act of desperation and aggression: "She realized that he did not expose his weapon by accident, but displayed it as if it were a war trophy in order to give himself courage. He did not even give her time to take off the nightgown that she had put on [. . .]. When it was over, however, she felt empty" (340). Why does García Márquez frame the novel this way? Does this frame support Booker's assertion (in question 6) about *Love* as a deceptively seductive story? How do these moments help explain Florentino's history with women?

(8) Fermina Daza is devastated by the slanderous articles published in *Justice*, a local tabloid committed to eroding the status of the aristocracy. In many ways, these articles raise questions about truth in storytelling. García Márquez specifically seems to be criticizing the ways in which people tend to believe what they read or see on television without question. At what other moments in the novel does misinformation and deception have devastating consequences? What is problematic about Florentino's missives for "unlettered lovers"? What do these letters imply about the relationships between those who request them?

(9) *Love in the Time of Cholera* opens with a suicide. Jeremiah de Saint-Amour kills himself in order to escape the humiliations of aging. As he explained to his lover, "he had made the irrevocable decision to take his own life when he was sixty years old" (15). Most of the characters fear aging. As Florentino ponders, "he was never as afraid of death as he was reaching that humiliating age when he would have to be led on a woman's arm. On that day, and only on that day, he knew he would have to renounce his hope of Fermina Daza" (257). Age, in other words, threatens one's dignity. How does the novel both counter and exacerbate such fears?

(10) Gene H. Bell-Villada notes that "erotica is depicted as delectable and positive for its own sake. To put it quite simply, Florentino

and his many bedmates enjoy each other without a trace of shame or guilt. Moreover, throughout *Love* it is the women who tend to take the initiative, and their aggressive, pantherlike sexuality is implicitly acclaimed rather than prudishly maligned" (197). Certainly, women celebrate the freedom that sexuality gives them. The Widow Nazaret, for example, thanks Florentino for their trysts in similar terms: "'I adore you because you made me a whore'" (151). What does she mean by this? How does Urbino fit into this portrayal of sexual desire? How does he respond to his own sexual desires?

(11) In the short novel *Chronicle of a Death Foretold*, García Márquez tells a love story in the context of detective fiction. In this murder "mystery," however, the typical order of events is reversed, and the identity of the criminals is revealed in the first chapter. In what ways does *Love in the Time of Cholera* play with the conventions of the suspense novel? How does Florentino invoke this tradition and why does García Márquez have him do so?

(12) Political strife clearly impacts the world of the novel, but the central characters seem apolitical in many ways. Urbino, for example, "defined himself as a natural pacifist, a partisan of definitive reconciliation between Liberals and Conservatives for the good of the nation" (44). And Fermina and her father survive one threat by not aligning with either party: "the assailants had awakened him with a rifle in his stomach, and a commander in rags, his face smeared with charcoal, had shone a light on him and asked him if he was Liberal or Conservative. 'Neither one or the other,' said Lorenzo Daza. 'I am a Spanish subject.' 'What luck! said the commander, and he left with his hand raised in a salute. 'Long live the King!'" (84). How does this rejection of partisan politics effect Fermina's and Urbino's relationship with the community? Is García Márquez advocating this kind of apolitical stance? Does the novel present any characters who are politically as well as socially responsible? If not, why not?

(13) Early in the novel, a woman who cleans rooms at a brothel describes the remnants of love:

It was difficult to imagine the number of things that men left after love. They left vomit and tears, which seemed understandable to her, but they also left many enigmas of intimacy: puddles of blood, patches of excrement, glass eyes, gold watches, false teeth, lockets with golden curls, love letters, business letters, condolence letters—all kinds of letters. Some came back for the items they had lost, but most were unclaimed, and Lotario Thugut kept them under lock and key and thought that sooner or later the palace that had seen better days, with its thousands of forgotten belongings, would become a museum of love. (77–8)

In many respects, this novel is about loss. Both men and women give up part of themselves for love. How are the sacrifices that men make for love different from those made by women? The housekeeper in this passage is puzzled by what remains after love. On a physiological level, the male body loses control after this act. It leaves behind fluids, blood, and excrement. This physical breakdown is also accompanied by sentimental losses, such as letters and lockets of hair. How are these sentimental losses essential for male desire?

(14) At one point, Florentino explains to his uncle that he cannot write a business letter: "'Love is the only thing that interests me,' he said. 'The trouble,' his uncle said to him, 'is that without river navigation there is no love'" (168). What does this mean? How is technology linked to love in the novel? Can you read both the condition of Riverboat Company and its impact on the land as a metaphor for love? Is the novel suggesting that love is ultimately selfish and destructive? Or is the text asking us to read love as a salve for the dangers of technology, disease, political violence, and aging?

Bibliography

1. BOOKS

In English Translation

The Autumn of the Patriarch. Translated by Gregory Rabassa. New York: Harper & Row, 1976.

Chronicle of a Death Foretold. Translated by Gregory Rabassa. New York: Alfred A. Knopf, 1982.

Clandestine in Chile: The Adventures of Miguel Littín. Translated by Asa Zatz. New York: Henry Holt, 1987.

Collected Stories. Translated by Gregory Rabassa and J. S. Bernstein. New York: Harper & Row, 1984.

The Fragrance of Guava: Plinio Apuleio Mendoza in Conversation with Gabriel García Márquez. Translated by Ann Wright. London: Verso, 1983.

The General in His Labyrinth. Translated by Edith Grossman. New York: Alfred A. Knopf, 1990.

In Evil Hour. Translated by Gregory Rabassa. New York: Harper & Row, 1979.

Leaf Storm and Other Stories. Translated by Gregory Rabassa. New York: Harper & Row, 1972.

Love in the Time of Cholera. Translated by Edith Grossman. New York: Alfred A. Knopf, 1988.

News of a Kidnapping. Translated by Edith Grossman. New York: Alfred A. Knopf, 1997.

No One Writes to the Colonel and Other Stories. Translated by J. S. Bernstein. New York: Harper & Row, 1968.

Of Love and Other Demons. Translated by Edith Grossman. New York: Alfred A. Knopf, 1995.

One Hundred Years of Solitude. Translated by Gregory Rabassa. New York: Avon Books, 1979.

The Story of a Shipwrecked Sailor. Translated by Randolph Hogan. New York: Alfred A. Knopf, 1986.

Strange Pilgrims. Translated by Edith Grossman. New York: Alfred A. Knopf, 1994.

2. BOOKS, ESSAYS, AND REVIEWS (SELECT)

Anderson, Jon Lee. "The Power of Gabriel García Márquez." *The New Yorker*, 27 September 1999: 56–69.

Bell-Villada, Gene H. *García Márquez: The Man and His Work*. Chapel Hill: The University of North Carolina Press, 1990.

Bloom, Harold, ed. *Modern Critical Views: Gabriel García Márquez*. New York: Chelsea House Publishers, 1989.

Booker, M. Keith. "The Dangers of Gullible Reading: Narrative as Seduction in García Márquez's *Love in the Time of Cholera*." *Studies in Twentieth Century Literature*, 17.2 (1993): 181–195.

Buehrer, David. "A Second Chance on Earth': The Postmodern and the Post-Apocalyptic in García Márquez's *Love in the Time of Cholera*." *Critique: Studies in Contemporary Fiction*, 32.1 (1990): 15–26.

Castronovo, David. "Love in the Time of Cholera." *America*, 10 September 1988: 146–8.

Clemmons, Walter. "The Sweet Plague of Love." *Newsweek*, 25 April 1988: 60–1.

Couteau, Robert. "Love in the Time of Cholera." *Arete Magazine*, December 1988. http://members.tripod.com/more_couteau/marquez.htm.

Fiddian, Robin. "A Prospective Post-Script: Apropos of *Love in the Time of Cholera*." *Gabriel García Márquez: New Readings*: 191–205.

Garcia Marquez, Gabriel. "The Solitude of Latin America." Rpt. in *Gabriel García Márquez: New Readings*: 207–11.

Hamill, Pete. "Love and Solitude." *Vanity Fair*, March 1988: 124–31.

Martinez-Maldonado, Manuel. "Numbers, Death, and Time in García Márquez's *Love in the Time of Cholera.*" *The Body and the Text: Comparative Essays in Literature and Medicine*. Eds. Bruce Clarke and Wendell Aycock. Lubbock: Texas Tech University Press, 1990: 127–37.

McGuirk, Bernard and Richard Cardwell, eds. *Gabriel García Márquez: New Readings*. Cambridge, Mass: Cambridge University Press, 1987.

McHale, Brian. *Postmodernist Fiction*. New York: Routledge, 1987.

Moraña, Mabel. "Modernity and Marginality in *Love in the Time of Cholera.*" *Studies in Twentieth Century Literature*, 14.1 (Winter 1990): 27–43.

"The Novel as Tropical Flower." *The Economist*, 2 July 1988: 77–8.

Penuel, Arnold M. *Intertextuality in García Márquez*. South Carolina: Spanish Literature Publications Company, 1994.

Winterson, Jeanette. *The Passion*. New York: Vintage, 1987.

———. *Sexing the Cherry*. New York: Vintage, 1989.

Zamora, Lois Parkinson, and Wendy B. Faris, eds. *Magical Realism: Theory, History, Community*. Durham: Duke University Press, 1995.

1122420

Made in the USA